Don't Swallow The Testicles

What Have You Been Missing?

Written
By
Kevin Roche

TRAFFORD

© Copyright 2005 Kevin Roche.
All rights reserved. No part of this publication may be reproduced, stored in a retrieval system, or transmitted, in any form or by any means, electronic, mechanical, photocopying, recording, or otherwise, without the written prior permission of the author.

Note for Librarians: a cataloguing record for this book that includes Dewey Decimal Classification and US Library of Congress numbers is available from the Library and Archives of Canada. The complete cataloguing record can be obtained from their online database at:
www.collectionscanada.ca/amicus/index-e.html
ISBN 1-4120-4554-1

Printed in Victoria, BC, Canada

Printed on paper with minimum 30% recycled fibre. Trafford's print shop runs on "green energy" from solar, wind and other environmentally-friendly power sources.

TRAFFORD
Offices in Canada, USA, Ireland and UK

This book was published *on-demand* in cooperation with Trafford Publishing. On-demand publishing is a unique process and service of making a book available for retail sale to the public taking advantage of on-demand manufacturing and Internet marketing. On-demand publishing includes promotions, retail sales, manufacturing, order fulfilment, accounting and collecting royalties on behalf of the author.

Book sales for North America and international:
Trafford Publishing, 6E–2333 Government St.,
Victoria, BC v8t 4p4 CANADA
phone 250 383 6864 (toll-free 1 888 232 4444)
fax 250 383 6804; email to orders@trafford.com

Book sales in Europe:
Trafford Publishing (uk) Ltd., Enterprise House, Wistaston Road Business Centre,
Wistaston Road, Crewe, Cheshire cw2 7rp UNITED KINGDOM
phone 01270 251 396 (local rate 0845 230 9601)
facsimile 01270 254 983; orders.uk@trafford.com

Order online at:
trafford.com/04-2362

10   9   8   7   6   5   4   3   2

My Beautiful Daughter Kate
One Without Guile

Contents

Introduction 7

1 In the Beginning was the Word
　and the Word was Testicles 10

2 Addictions 17

3 Thank you for Your Vote,
　Now we'll do What we Like 33

4 Here is Your Daily Dose of Fear 47

5 Don't Prosecute Yourself 55

6 Testicles Won't Make You Look Younger 60

7 Unreality Television 66

8 What Are You Putting Into Your Body? 71

9 Questionnaires, Surveys and
　Loyalty Reward Cards 76

10 So You're In Love, Are You? 81

11 If You Keep Doing What You're Doing
　 You'll Keep Getting What You're Getting 88

Introduction

"When are you going to write that book?" That's what I've been saying to myself for far too long. It's amazing how I've put it off and drip-fed myself all kinds of excuses for doing so. That is why there has been a lengthy delay in getting this book into your hands. I apologise and hope that the delay hasn't prolonged your misery too much. One of my close friends said to me, "The cure for procrastination Kevin, is DO IT NOW". So let's waste no more time, let's write.

I have strong views about the topics covered in this book and at times my tongue is not in my cheek and at other times it is only partially in my cheek when making many of my comments. During the past couple of years I've seen autobiographies, of so-called celebrities who are only in their twenties and thirties, on sale in the shops. What is someone doing writing their life story when they are still so young? They haven't had a life yet. Being pissed up, doped up and shagging your way into the media spotlight can hardly be called a life. Being promoted to fame and succeeding at living life are two completely different things. It's okay to have fame so long as it is used for completely unselfish good causes. That means don't do good deeds and hope that they might result in you being rewarded.

Autobiographies should all have the title My Story So Far, because our lives are not over until we draw our very last breath.

One day I awakened to the realisation that I was living in

DON'T SWALLOW THE TESTICLES

a country and probably a world with millions of people who are treated like sheep and have fodder fed to them every day of the week. Much of it is fed to them by the media who use a whole network of suppliers who queue in droves to get themselves on television and in newspapers to justify what they do. I believe that this fodder feeding starts at a very early age and can continue throughout life.

The sheep-people are those who go through life with their eyes semi closed and swallow all the fodder that is fed to them. They're docile and the shepherds see no reason to change them. Let's face it, they're easier to manipulate in that state.

It was after much thought that I decided to give this fodder the name of TESTICLES. I believe this to be an apt name for it. TESTICLES have been around for a long time so they're quite old.

"Don't Swallow The Testicles" is not a book about oral sex. It is a signpost pointing towards some of the sources of TESTICLES. The people who feed us their fodder of testicles do so by invading our minds and taking over our thinking so that they can control us and promote their own disguised agendas. Their methods work in much the same way as pop ups, ad ware and spy ware invading our computers. Many sprinkle their fodder with lashings of fear and if swallowed can cause problems with our health, our wealth and our happiness.

WAKE UP! The time has come for you to take ownership of your mind. Throw away your excuse books. You can't rebuild your past but you can build your future. Let today be the first day of the best of your life. Are you aware of anyone who gets up in the mornings and asks themselves what they can do today to improve your life? The fact is that it's all up to you to make your life the best that it can possibly be. You really don't need anyone's permission to create the life you want for yourself. Don't listen to the dream stealers, they will transfer all their excuses onto you as to why you can't ever be successful. You don't need money and degrees, the only two things that you need are belief in yourself and a good measure of audacity.

This book may disturb you, with its critical hard-hitting ruthlessness for truth, but it can also set you on the path to freedom, health and happiness. The message that I am offering you is that in this life misery is optional.

Grab this message with both hands and follow me through the pages of my book. The things that seem important will become unimportant and the things that seem unimportant will become important. Life will take on a new meaning for you. Your imagination will be fired and you will never be the same again.

DON'T SWALLOW THE TESTICLES

1
In the Beginning was the Word and the Word was Testicles

Were you told the story about Adam and Eve in the Garden of Eden with the apple and the snake? Did you ever check the story out to find out if it was a true story? No one was there to witness it. No one was there to write it down. No one was there taking minutes. We don't know what language they spoke and yet we were told that they did speak. Surely these observations make those events just a tiny bit suspect. Yet, with this story as its foundation, millions of sheep-people have been fed the testicles of Christian religion that when they die they will be transported to another life that will be their just reward for toeing the line whilst they were here missing out on this life.

Can you imagine your fifteen-year old daughter coming home and announcing that she was pregnant and then telling you, "she hadn't had sex with a boy behind the bike shed, she had been impregnated by a holy spirit". You'd believe her story, wouldn't you? Christian religion has been feeding the world a line like this for hundreds of years and the sheep-people have believed it.

What would you say if a bloke carrying a tool bag approached you in the street today and said, "I'm a carpenter and I want you to leave everything and follow me, I will make you a fisher of people and we will wander all over the country together"?

DON'T SWALLOW THE TESTICLES

Leave everything! You mean my family, home, job, car, mobile phone, DVD, PC, TV, designer clothes, and friends. Testicles! Fuck off.

The bible depicts those in authority as the villains and abusers of people. This carpenter from Nazareth is presented as someone who refused to allow himself to be seduced by the status quo of the day. I don't know about you but I find those words very refreshing. This carpenter was someone who obviously had ownership of his own mind. In the New Statement he is only mentioned at his birth then again when he is twelve and finally there is a three year period of ministry that began when he was thirty. What happened to him for eighteen years? If the accounts of what he said are true then it would seem that during his three year period of ministry he said very little. How much have you said during the last three years?

The deviously manufactured bible seems to be a book about good and bad, right and wrong, success and failure, fear and guilt and should be read with a mature eye. I believe in a Higher Power who only wants one club, without rules and laws, and membership of it open to everyone. I also believe that this Higher Power wants us to focus on life this side of death and not concern ourselves with a life on the other side of it. I do not hold with the Christian belief that God can be kept under lock and key in a tabernacle and made available only to the conformist.

I don't see why the bible is used in our law courts when people are sworn in as witnesses. People who may never have stepped foot inside of a church step into a witness box and say "I swear by almighty God…" It is highly unlikely that most people are bothered anymore about the wrath of God and we know today that truth means different things to different people. What about witnesses who are not so-called Christians? What about those people who are frightened to give evidence and are allowed to do so via video links? They obviously don't believe in putting faith in a God who they can't see.

Many Christian infant schools continue to re-enact the nativity play in December. So it goes on year after year, the singing of carols by the old and the young, the same old testicles being passed from one generation to another. I don't hear the old singing nursery rhymes, they were taught them as children too. They give the nursery rhymes up but not the carols. They cling to the religion thing because it's the familiar.

Were you brought up and fed a diet of Christian religion? Have you considered taking a fresh look at your belief system? As children we had to accept what we were told, we didn't really have a choice. Most of what our parents passed onto us was stuff that had been passed onto them by their parents. What are you passing on? Who is going to break the chain?

Do you still speak like a child and act like a child? Do you still believe in Father Christmas, The Easter Bunny and the Tooth Fairy? Put away childish things and GROW UP.

One day a mother sent her son to the butchers for a leg of lamb, "Make sure you get the end cut off", she said. Her son returned home with the leg of lamb and asked his mother, "Why do we always get the butcher to cut the end off?" His mother replied, "We always have done. My mother did it and my grandmother did it". Her son went to see his grandmother and discovered that the reason why his great grandmother always had the end cut off a leg of lamb was because she only had a small oven. (Author Unknown)

Ways of doing things will continue to be passed on if they go unquestioned. Get in the habit of questioning everything.

Thankfully, Christian religion has lost its grip on many people. It is no longer a case of leaving the ninety-nine and going out after the one, it's more a case of leaving the one and going out after the ninety-nine. Some of the main Christian religions lost their credibility because of issues concerning gay clergy, the ordination of women to the priesthood and paedophile priests. For years they ignored the rot that was spreading through their masquerade and it eventually collapsed and left them exposed. The sheep now have Garden Centres and DIY Shops to pay homage to on Sundays anyway. That seems to be much more fun.

Have you noticed how the Christian churches are conspicuous by their silence during a time when thousands of innocent men, women and children are being slaughtered in various parts of the world? One of the main Christian religions has created a convenient diversion to focus their attention on concerning women and gay priests being promoted to bishops. Instead of the Christian churches leading the world they are allowing themselves to be led by the world.

Some of the fugitive sheep pop back to church now and again, just to make payments on their fire insurance. A few pop back when they need a recommendation from the priest to get their child into a religious school. Others might make only three visits during their lifetime, baptism, marriage and death, or if you like, hatch, match and dispatch.

I know this guy, he appears to be quite bright and clever and well put together but he has a little problem that has been going on for years. He never goes to church but whenever he goes

DON'T SWALLOW THE TESTICLES

back home to Ireland he has to go to church with his mother. She thinks that he goes to church every week but he is too afraid to tell her that he doesn't. He is in his fifties and still behaving like a little boy. He still has a childhood fear that he must let go of if he wants to step onto the road to freedom.

Sometime ago a lady called at my house. She belongs to one of those door-knocking religions. She said to me, "Do you ever feel lonely?" I said, "No". She said, "Have you ever been in a crowd and felt lonely?" I said, "No". She said, "Do any members of your family ever feel lonely?" I said, "No". She said, "I feel lonely sometimes, even when I'm in a crowd". I said, "I can see why". I then said to her, "Look I don't want to waste your time, I really don't believe in all this stuff". She thanked me and moved on. I noticed at the front gate there were five or six other disciples, with kids in pushchairs, waiting for her. What a way to spend a lovely sunny day. I can just imagine her giving those old testicles about being lonely to other people and them joining in with it.

More recently a "Christian Aid Week" envelope was put through my front door letterbox. The following week one of my neighbours knocked on the door and said "I'm collecting the Christian Aid Week envelopes that were delivered last week". I informed him that I had put it in the dustbin and he offered me another one. I said, "I don't give to Christian Aid".

There was a time when I would have put money in that envelope because I wouldn't have wanted my neighbour to think that I was unchristian or a tight fisted bastard. Today I know that is people pleasing and I don't engage in it. Today I have a set of strong life principles and I say what I believe and not what I think others want to hear.

Christian religions are right-wing businesses and like any other business they are out to make money. The commodity they promote is called salvation. To them the word prophet is spelt PROFIT. Like other businesses they have competitors and have to think of ways to promote their particular brand of religion and some are proficient at doing that. They discovered long ago that if you get a customer at a very young age and handle them properly then there is a good chance of keeping that person as a member of your customer family for life. That's good business sense. What other business do you know that has been going for hundreds of years and only focuses on an end product that no one can prove whether or not anyone actually gets? What a fantastic money maker.

From America now comes The Silver Ring Crusade. It involves a New Age Religion Movement who are brainwashing young girls into saving their virginity until they are married. The girls have to buy the silver ring and it is placed on their finger during a ceremony. This is nothing more than an updated version of mugging with a religious face to it.

Out of Africa is emerging an evangelical movement that is giving its founder a very comfortable life style. What a great way to make a living. Just feed testicles to the susceptible and they will part with their money week after week.

If religion isn't making you happy then free yourself from its constraining hold on you. THE REAL KINGDOM IS WITHIN YOU not outside of you. Don't make someone or something outside of yourself responsible for what happens in your life. That includes governments, praying, meditation, yoga, psychics, clairvoyance, horoscopes, tarot cards, palmistry, numerology, runes, and all that other testicles. The greatest power of all is to have ownership of your mind. Believe in yourself and take responsibility for your life and then great things will happen to you. Amen.

I'm sure there will be people who read what I have said and will scream, "Heresy, he will burn in the fires of hell for this". I understand. You see, I've been on the inside of Christian religion and I've seen those people clinging to the altar railings with their mouths hung open for a little wafer. Nowadays many of them have grey hair, white hair or no hair and they tend to be unhappy and consumed with shame, guilt and resentment. Invite these people to change their belief system and they will accuse you of doing the devils work. I used to think that the glint in the eyes of some professed Christians was charisma but today I believe that it could be psychosis.

I have also seen priests hiding behind white collars and living out quiet lives of desperation within the walls of presbyteries. Many of these guys are "control freaks" and they harbour great resentment towards their Bishops who they feel do not support them. Some of them die quite young but don't get buried until they're quite old. Like so many other people they die inwardly. A Bishop once said to me "Kevin, I don't think that the church is ready for someone like you yet". I said to him "the church may not be ready but the people might be".

Many people live in the, If only world. "If only I'd said this". "If only I'd done that". "If only this had happened". Don't be one of these people. Don't live a life of nostalgia. Let go of times that cannot return and give your energy to those things that produce the greatest results. The person who has been blessed with the gift of hindsight has been blessed with nothing.

2
Addictions

Today we have among us, alcoholics, food addicts, gambling addicts, men addicts, women addicts, dope addicts, and soap addicts. If I have missed anyone out then I apologise. I shall be giving you my views on these addictions but for now I want to say that I believe the underlying cause of all addiction is SELF-WILL. You can disagree with my simple diagnosis as much as you want but I will stand by it.

Many people today claim to be products of dysfunctional families. I don't believe there is such a thing. Somewhere along the line this term was invented and sheep-people seized on it and decided this was the reason for their crap lives. Let's get the hankies out and have a good cry for them. There are a great number of people making money from feeding these poor self-pitying sheep the dysfunctional family testicles.

Therapist, counsellors, writers, life coaches or whatever other name they might go by have really created an industry for themselves. What about those TV presenters who get an audience of sheep-people every weekday and feed them testicles? What another great way to make a living? No shortage of sheep-people either. "If you have a problem with your weight, phone us now". Within seconds the phone lines are jammed and a few days later they're in the audience bleating about how their lives are in a mess because of all the crap food they've shoved into their mouths. What about all the testicles

DON'T SWALLOW THE TESTICLES

they come out with for doing it? "My relationship broke up". "My mother is an alcoholic". My father didn't love me when I was a child". Don't go on TV and give the whole nation your self-pitying drivel. Stop cramming crap food into your mouth and make the decision to change. Make a decision don't hold a discussion.

Sometime ago I watched a young girl on one of those shows describe how her boyfriend had beat her up several times and on three occasions had put her in hospital. The presenter introduced the girl's boyfriend to the audience and as he made his way onto the stage they applauded him. What message did they send to that guy? Another guy on one of those programmes was crying and blaming his parents for his messed up life. He told the presenter that he was sixty-three!

It seems fashionable to be "an addict" today. Who minds? It is well catered for. If you commit crime to get drugs and get caught there is a good chance that you will be sent to a nice treatment centre. There you will be placed on a strict diet of testicles and fed things like you have a little child within you that you need to locate and make friends with. What a load of self-pitying testicles? On the testicle scale of one to ten this gets a big TEN.

There are some sheep-people who actually consider it fashionable to have a therapist. GET A FUCKING LIFE!

On my way home in the car just before Christmas I was listening to a radio station and the presenter said, "After the break we will be joined by a Christmas therapist who is going to tell us how to get through Christmas". What another load of testicles. I quickly changed stations.

Go into most bookshops and you will find no end of "How To …" books. This market is worth millions of £££s. Many sheep-people buy these books hoping to find ways to break out of their pens. They take the books home, read them and then continue to swallow the fodder that is served to them. Why do you suppose that is? The reason is because they don't really want to change. By the way, I once read a manual called "How to Write How to Books". Does that tell you something about these books?

Did you know there are sports clubs and companies that hire motivational speakers to motivate the players and work force in the hope that they will perform better? There is only one way that they are going to perform better and it really isn't a secret. It is a tried and tested and proven method that guarantees a minimum 5% improvement (increasing more as the person develops) from every player or employee and employer. You don't need to be a mathematician to work out that a single employer with a work force of just nineteen can get a minimum 100% overall improvement from their workforce. No one can motivate someone else; people can only do it to themselves, though it is possible to shine a light through the cracks and start the process. It really is a case of the right words from the right person at the right time. It is my hope that this book contains the right words and that I am the right person and that the right time for you is NOW.

Motivational speaking is big business. There are some guys who can get hundreds of sheep-people to attend a weekend motivational workshop and dazzle them for thirty-six hours. The sheep-people pay up to a £1000 each to attend the event and they leave on a great high on Sunday. By Wednesday they're deflated and back to feeling the same way they did before the weekend. The speaker has returned home, probably to the USA, with his bank balance well and truly inflated, he's got

DON'T SWALLOW THE TESTICLES

a workshop for another flock of sheep people the following weekend. I've listened to many motivational tapes and I've read many motivational books and I discovered that they say a great deal but tell you very little.

Don't get drawn into the motivation testicles. Real everlasting change always involves taking inner action followed by outer action. It's about changing habits. If you always put your coat on right arm first, start doing it left arm first, left sock and shoe first instead of right sock and shoe. You need to break the way that you have always done things. The book you need is now in your hands, study it, don't just read through it once and then put it to one side, use it as a textbook, consult it often and make notes in the back section. If you take what you learn here and only use it as knowledge it will gain you very little. If you turn what you learn here into action you will reap great rewards.

Let's keep it simple. Many sheep-people who visit a therapist have only two conditions. They are self-centred and fully paid up members of the self-pity committee. Their state stems from testicles that were fed to them by someone at some stage during their lives.

The therapist assures the emotional cripple that they can be helped and embarks on a course of weekly sessions. Three months and twelve session fees later the sheep-person is still the same. Why is that? It's because they have probably been fed more testicles during those three months. The best advice to give this person is, take a trip down to the local hospice and see if you can help out there. *"I complained because I had no shoes then I met a man who had no feet"*. (Author Unknown).

You see I don't really want to hear about what you've been

through. I'm more interested in hearing about how you intend to turn your stumbling blocks into stepping stones.

I remember this guy who asked for my help. I met him one day and he was looking glum. I said "What's up with you today?" He said, "I've got parent problems". I said to him, "I don't know what you're talking about and I don't want to know otherwise I might get them". He never tried to feed me that load of testicles again.

This guy had been to one of those treatment centres for alcoholism and had been fed this stuff about his parents. He should have had it pointed out to him that he was the one in the treatment centre not his parents. Why do so many people waste such a vast amount of their lives trying to get on with their parents? Who said that you have to get on with your parents anyway? Getting on with yourself is much more important and if you learn to laugh at yourself there will never be a dull moment.

Some of the sheep-people go bonkers now and then and they end up in treatment centres where they sit in groups with other sheep-people who have also gone bonkers and they try to cure each other. They say things like, "I had to deal with anger on Monday when I was kept waiting at the doctors for my sick certificate" or "someone at home left the top off the toothpaste". The group spend the next hour discussing this guy's earth shattering experience. At the end of these sessions they hold hands and say, "Keep coming back". Isn't therapy a wonderful thing?

Now, you might be thinking, "It's alright for this bloke to knock all this nice convenient excuse making stuff, I bet he had a good childhood with wonderful loving parents". WRONG. I had no such thing. I was one of nine children with an alcoholic violent father. The NSPCC, Police and Welfare Services were regular visitors to our house. We were always being taken into protective care and on one occasion I was taken to be photographed because my body was covered in criss-cross patterns made by a belt. My father was sent to prison for cruelty to his children following, what was for us, a six-year reign of terror by him.

There is no way that I would jump on the dysfunctional family bandwagon because of my childhood experiences.

I can hear the therapists saying, "He's in denial". To which I say, TESTICLES.

You see, I believe that if I had missed just one of my life's many experiences I would not be where I am today on my wonderful journey of discovery. I could have gone through life hating my father but that may have destroyed me and not him. My father wasn't a bad man; he just wasn't a good father.

Now here's an excellent tip. Please heed it. Avoid alcohol. Why go into a bar and order a glass of brain damage? If you are going to persist in doing this then on future visits to the bar do the following three things, the third one will cut you out as the middle man.

1. Order your drink.
2. Pay for your drink.
3. Ask the barman to take it out to the toilet and pour it down the bowl.

Have a nice refreshing glass of sparkling water instead. I love chilled sparkling water; it's wonderful. Drinking sparkling water will not get you into a fight or locked up or lose you your driving licence or get you taken to the A&E Department or have you holding onto the toilet bowl whilst retching into it or make you mistake the dirty linen basket and the wardrobe for the toilet or prevent you from getting up in the mornings. Do you see some of the benefits?

Today we have so-called professionals who use terms such as "alcohol abuse" and "alcohol misuse" to explain away unacceptable behaviour from people who are drunk due to their drinking being out of control. The reason they are drunk is because of "alcohol use", nothing else. There is now a new term, "Binge Drinking". What a load of testicles. Not so many years ago the term was "Lager Louts" and the Government failed to apply correct methods to deal with the problem and it therefore remained. There are thousands of "Binge Drinkers" pouring out onto the streets in towns and cities across the country and causing mayhem. It's insanity and its real name is ALCOHOLISM. Why are the police being used to police insanity? Surely this behaviour should be policed by staff from the mental health services.

Do normal drinkers say "I'm going to get wrecked" or "rat arsed" or "out of my head" or "blitzed"? Many people make these statements and proceed to carry them out. If you are one of these people then I suggest that you have a serious booze problem that you are choosing to ignore. Chances are that you handle the first few drinks and the ones that follow handle you. Write down all the good things that happen to you during and following a drinking session.

The number one symptom of alcoholism is denial and the Government is in denial about the extent of this colossal health problem. In fact they think that the answer might be all day drinking. If they apply this solution to the problem it won't cost them any money. The Government is also addicted to

DON'T SWALLOW THE TESTICLES

the colossal revenue that the sale of alcohol generates. Many politicians like a drop of brain damage themselves and quite a few are in denial about their own drinking habits. Part of the insanity of this problem is that it tends to get dealt with by people who drink.

If you want to stop drinking and find that you can't then seek help. If your drinking is costing you more than money then seek help. If you are trying to drink your whole life's quota in one night then seek help. Don't waste your time visiting alcohol advice centres they have their own agendas and are too concerned with their image and how they can get more funding.

One of my friends shares a story about going to an alcohol advice centre. The advice he was given by one of the counsellors was that the next time he went into a pub he should make sure that he had some loose change on him. Each time he had a drink he should transfer a coin from one pocket to the other and when he had three coins in his other pocket he should leave the pub and go home. What a load of testicles. There is no way an alcoholic is going home after three drinks. Three drinks have only just lit the fire. An alcoholic needs to know and understand that it's the first drink that does the damage. Don't take the first drink and you won't get drunk. Those ten simple words have baffled the famous, geniuses, scientists and many other people of high intelligence.

If you want to stop drinking, not cut it down but cut it out, then the best help that is available and free is Alcoholics Anonymous; look them up in your phone book. It is better to be sat in an A.A. meeting pretending to be an alcoholic than to be sat in some bar pretending that you are not one. The Twelve Step Programme of Recovery will free you from your false love affair with booze and will turn your life around completely because it treats the whole person. If you decide that it's not for you then you can leave and keep your misery.

If you are living with a drunk then you need help too. The best help can be found at Al-Anon meetings. Find out where they meet and get yourself along there. Al-Anon members say, "You don't have to drink to suffer from alcoholism". Many of these people have presented themselves at the doctors, as the sick one, while the alcoholic in their life has continued drinking. It is impossible to live with a practising alcoholic and not be affected by their drinking and behaviour. Perhaps you have found yourself demanding answers to some of the following illogical questions.

- "Who do you think you are?"
- "What time do you call this?"
- "What do you take me for?"
- "I've had it up to here with you"
- "If you loved me you wouldn't do it"
- "What about me, don't I matter?"

If you are in a relationship with a drunk and you are putting up with the insanity that comes from such a situation then there is more wrong with you than you might care to admit. It isn't the alcoholic that you should be addressing questions to; you should be addressing questions to yourself. So go to Al-Anon and hopefully you will learn a great deal about yourself.

Alcohol is a big problem in the work place also. Many people cover up for drunks at work, the reason being is that many of the work force like a drink themselves. There is no bigger danger than a drunk in the work place. If you know of one then have the courage to bring that person to the attention of the management. Management should have the courage to call

DON'T SWALLOW THE TESTICLES

the drunk before them and if the information is true tell him or her to seek help or seek new employment. No other words are necessary.

STOP DRINKING ALCOHOL AND START LIVING. DO IT NOW. How can you have ownership of your mind with artificial stimulants in your body? If you want to get high then get high on life; that is the greatest stimulant of all.

Don't run off at the mouth here and say, "It's alright for him he's probably never had a drink in his life". I don't drink but there was a time when I did and it was TROUBLE all the way. On the 25th May 1981 I picked up the phone and made the call that was to change my life. The guy on the other end of the phone asked me just one question, "Do you want to stop drinking?" I said, "Yes". One day at a time I am approaching my twenty-forth year of sobriety. I didn't go to one of those treatment centres so I didn't get sidetracked with that "little child within" testicles. If I can do it then anyone can do it. Take a good look at yourself in the mirror; you are now looking at the problem. Really look at yourself. Don't just brush your teeth or comb your hair or put your make up on. We look in the mirror every day but fail to see ourselves as we really are.

When I say to people, "I don't drink" they often say, "Not even at Christmas", I then have to repeat my statement to them on account of them having defective hearing.

What is an alcoholic? Quite simply it is a person for whom alcohol is in charge. The definition is in the word. ALCOHOL + IC. IC stands for In Charge = Alcohol in Charge. You don't need qualifications to diagnose the condition you just need a pair of eyes. This definition is too easy for the experts it won't get them grants, they would rather hold a series of focus groups and draw up a funded five-year programme of testicles to deal with the problem. An alcoholic could be someone who only drinks once every ten or so years. If the first drink sets up the craving for more then that person is an alcoholic.

It can be easy to stop drinking but many find it hard to stay stopped. The media has highlighted this fact so often in its reporting of alcoholic so-called celebrities. The truth is that these guys didn't want to stop drinking, they love being in the news and telling their self-pitying stories about "My Battle with the Bottle" but they have never got down to dealing with the underlying symptoms of their drinking and they continue to suffer from untreated alcoholism. The absence of alcohol usually reveals a messy background that the alcoholic needs to clean up.

The media and these publicity junkies have a co-dependent relationship with each other. They are supplier and pusher of a drug that they both desperately need. That drug is called publicity.

For years the media have been obsessed with a has-been footballer who hasn't wanted to stop drinking full time. The guy is the town sot the local drunk; leave him alone in peace to drink himself to death.

So, let me now tell you how I see some of those other addictions. By the way, if you want to find out if you are addicted to something just try giving it up for a month. You see how easy the solutions are to most of life's situations? You don't need someone to carry out an assessment on you, you can assess yourself.

Drug Addiction: Massive self-inflicted problem. Too much help available for those taking drugs. There is too much funding being given to so-called professionals to tackle and treat the problem. Throwing money at the problem is not the way to solve it. This can create an income dependency from drugs for the so-called professionals.

Drug addiction has created a huge increase in crime of every description. Minimum sentence for committing crime to get drugs should be five years. Perhaps the new laws on home intruders will trim some of the drug addict population. There are no mitigating (testicles) circumstances. If no one took drugs there would be no pushers or suppliers. Solicitors and Barristers should not seek to turn drug addicts into victims when they appear in the courts. Why is there always a rush to make unacceptable behaviour acceptable? What about the victims of their crimes?

If drug addicts want to kill themselves on an instalment plan then let them, they made the decision. Why not take all the money that is spent to get addicts off the drugs that they chose to take and spend it on caring for the elderly in our society? Don't continue to shaft the elderly; they have contributed vastly to society.

Today, many of our older people can't even get their GP to visit them. What a disgrace. Perhaps GPs time is being taken up by drug addicts. Many elderly people when they don't feel very well contact their GP and get told "it's your age". What a poor excuse to fob a human being off with.

Food Addiction: Large self-inflicted and inflated problem leading to obesity. This person seeks food for comfort. They have little or no will power. They are members of the self-pity committee. They feel unwanted, unneeded and unloved. Some think that big is beautiful. If you really want to get rid of the excess weight that you chose to pile on then get up off your fat arse and search out Weapons of Mass Reduction.

Gambling Addiction: This individual has an obsession with betting. They get heavily into debt and sell everything to get money to gamble. This guy may or may not stop at some stage but I wouldn't bet on it. This guy is sure that he is going to clean out the bookie one day. The bookie has no need to worry because the next day it will be returned to him.

Men Addicts: Women who must be with a man. They can't be without one. They have never spent long enough, on their own, (Four years is a recommended period) to find out why. They tend to have unrealistic romanticised expectations and this makes them look for something from a man that he doesn't have. Their frustration at feeling let down makes them label men as being "emotionally unavailable", "robots" and "from Mars". This woman, because of her deep sense of insecurity, tends to be invasive and emotionally demanding. She needs constant tension in a relationship and she usually creates it when it isn't present. If a bloke tells this lady that he fancies her it's a guarantee that her knickers will be down around her ankles within minutes because she will give sex to feel loved. She tends to weep what she sows. She often repeats the same mistakes over and over again and finally decides that all men are the same and that she won't have any more to do with them. Just a minute though, he looks nice!

Women Addicts: Most men have this addiction. It is really sexual addiction. They see a woman they like the look of and they think "I'd love to shag that". That short skirt high up those beautiful legs with boots on them and that lovely little arse in those tight fitting jeans are called bait. Be warned, you maybe sticking your dick into a wet and warm trap that you might regret for a long time after.

Soap Addicts: These are very sad sheep-people. At the time of writing there are five soaps taking up twenty and a half hours a week on TV channels 1, 3, & 4. If you watch them all (then just for information) those hours amount to a little more than forty-four days a year. I went through a short phase once of following one of these soaps and soon realised that there was no one in it that was acting the part of someone who was happy. Perhaps that is what the sheep people identify with? Their own lives are just so miserable that they have to watch misery in order not to feel unique.

I once asked a woman why she liked a particular soap and she said, "It's just like real life". I think she meant that it was just like her life. Don't squander life. Find happiness within yourself and the soaps will hold no more appeal for you. Take ownership of your mind and feed it positive thoughts and work towards becoming successful with living life. You can do it. Believe that you can do it and you will Be Incredibly Great = BIG.

It was a privilege and a pleasure for me to read the stories of a number of well-known successful people. These people came from deprived backgrounds, they had poor schooling and never went to university and yet they made it to the top of their professions. They did not accept that because they had nothing as children that it would always be that way for them. They kept their gaze facing forward. They refused to dwell on the past. If you drive your car with your gaze firmly fixed in the rear view mirror it won't be long before you crash. These people have my greatest respect and admiration. It doesn't matter where you came from, what matters is where you want to go to.

We all come into the world with nothing and the majority keep most of it throughout their lives. They accept the testicles that are dished out to them and instead of living seventy or eighty years once they live one year seventy or eighty times. Why do so many people resent those who are successful? It's because they would like to be successful too but they swallowed the testicles and enslaved themselves. Do you notice how so many people seem to die when they're in their thirties but they don't get buried until they're in their seventies or eighties? Choose life. We are only coming through once. This is not a dummy run. Squeeze all the juice from it that you can. Make sure that the ladder you are climbing is up against the right wall.

We are living in a victim society today. Very few people will own up to being a culprit and take responsibility for their actions. Many people's decision making muscles have become flabby through lack of exercise. We have had so many restricting laws, rules and regulations imposed on us, by elected trusted servants, that people are frightened to make a decision in case it backfires on them. Signs like, "Where there's blame there's a claim" are displayed for all to see. Take a look in the classified phone book under solicitors; they're mostly interested in claim cases, obviously that is where money is to be made. Victims are coming out of the woodwork and suddenly remembering a little trip or slip they had during the past three years and they quickly become members of the addictive compensation culture. Perhaps this is why many people don't invite others into their homes anymore. What if they had an accident while they were there?

Are you beginning to catch hold of the message that I am

DON'T SWALLOW THE TESTICLES

sharing with you? If you can accept some large chunks of truth about yourself then you are soon going to be looking down the road that leads to freedom. Don't put this book down now. Keep following me. I'm soon going to be showing you more of the testicles that are dished out to us. Don't do anything about them other than not swallow them anymore. If you challenge them you will be served more of them. Be aware of them, make others aware of them but don't fight against them. Never try to teach sheep to sing because you only waste your time and it irritates the sheep.

I've had to let go of many things in my life and I can tell you that every time I've let go of something I've always found that the ground has been right underneath my feet. Believe me, there is no falling into some abyss that you can never return from. You really are still on your feet and just need to take ownership of your mind, move forward and don't look back, if you do, don't stare. Remember that a setback is an opportunity for a comeback.

3
Thank you for Your Vote, Now we'll do What we Like

What's the difference between all political parties? The answer is there is no difference. They all want the same thing. That thing is controlling power.

At this time of writing, the killing and abuse of thousands of innocent people has been continuing in Iraq. Why are they calling it a war? Who slipped that word in during the course of events? It was the unlawful invasion and overwhelming of vulnerable people by a superior force. Those who decided to defend their country against foreign invaders have been labelled as rebels, insurgents and terrorists.

Isn't it strange, television has shown us almost daily since the start of the invasion, people dying horrible deaths and being tortured in violent ways and homes being bombed and yet it hasn't been moving enough to start an aid appeal? Yet when we are shown people dying from aids, starvation or a tsunami, people are quick to respond with acts of overwhelming generosity. Surely dying in an awful way and losing homes is the same for the people of Iraq as it is for the people of Africa and Asia.

The British people were told by their Prime Minister that the reason for the invasion of Iraq was to prevent an evil dictator from using weapons of mass destruction. The dictator was captured on the 13th December 2003 and the alleged claims concerning weapons of mass destruction and links with terrorist organizations have turned out to be testicles. A Prime Minister who misleads a whole nation about such a grave matter would not hesitate to mislead them about anything. The Prime Minister has destroyed his own credibility and should never be trusted again.

The Prime Minister can't or won't apologise for getting it so disastrously wrong over Iraq. Can't apologise would indicate that he is stubborn. Won't apologise would indicate that he is arrogant. The fact is that he and the President of the USA are both responsible for every man, woman and child killed during the invasion and the ongoing occupation of Iraq.

The Prime Minister and the President both remain unrepentant about their decision to invade Iraq. In fact they both now think that the whole matter should be swept under the carpet and put behind us and that we should all now move forward in a spirit of unity. The President has recently described his invasion of Iraq as a fading past event. Well, let's adopt the same attitude about all the other atrocities that have been committed over the years. Does it really matter who was to blame? When members of our armed forces are killed in Iraq don't you find it nauseating when the Prime Minister goes on TV and gives a spiel about our thoughts and prayers are with the families?

We have had the findings of two inquiries concerning the role of the British government in the invasion of Iraq and both decided that no one individual was to blame for dishing out testicles that misled the people of Britain. I hope that no one was surprised to be told this.

Compare those inquiries with the one concerning the school caretaker child killer of Soham and the Humberside Police Force. They didn't declare no one to blame there. The Home Secretary pulled out all the stops to ensure that the Chief Constable was got rid of. The Home Secretary obviously didn't know that when you point the finger out you have three pointing back at yourself. "There are none as blind as those who cannot see". Let's hope that former Home Secretary now realises this.

Politicians are placed in positions of power by the electorate and then go off and do their own thing. They dictate rather than govern. They bring in laws that restrict and limit us and tell us that such measures are for our own good when in fact they are to control us and get more money from us to pay for their own impulsive acts of grandiosity. The promises they made when they wanted votes were just a load of testicles. They really don't give a toss what the so-called man in the street thinks.

There is no difference between the political parties. The bottom line is they are all in the same business. When one party is in power the other parties do all they can to discredit them? It appears that they can say what they like when they are in opposition.

They all want power and it is power that blinds them to the needs of people. They don't really see people, they see votes and that's what matters to them. If you believe that a government is acting in your interest then you still believe in that Tooth Fairy. Governments act in their own interests.

Have you noticed that politicians never give a straightforward yes or no answer to a question? Why is that? Is it because they can't very well twist such an answer around to mean something else at a later date? Have you also noticed that when they don't want to admit to something they say things like, "I can't recall having heard that", or "I can't recall having seen that" or "I think the real question is…" and then they answer their own question.

Have you also noticed how senior members in government avoid making decisions by setting up committees and inquiries to look into whatever it is that they want to avoid dealing with? This way they don't have to answer any more questions about the matter because it is the subject of an inquiry, which might take months before the findings are made known and many people will have forgotten by then what it was set up for in the first place.

Do you get pissed off with constantly hearing about the so-called power struggles that are supposed to go on within these political parties? Forgive me if I appear ignorant but I thought that these politicians were supposed to be running the country on behalf of the people. These devised ploys are designed to distract our focus away from real issues that government would rather we didn't take too much notice of.

What about when a government minister perceives a potential "banana skin" heading in his/her direction that they want to avoid? They suddenly resign and say the reason is to spend more time with their family and in their constituency. When the coast becomes clear again some of them get brought back into the inner circle and are given another audience to perform in front of.

Another ploy they use is when they want to introduce an increase in something it tends to first get "leaked". Suppose they wanted to increase VAT to 20%. They "leak" that VAT is going to rise to 25%. This causes uproar and the people take to the streets to protest. The government eventually relent and decide to increase VAT to only 20%. The people are convinced that it was their protests that made the government climb down.

You have probably seen those people who make up the audience on so-called political debate TV shows. Why do they waste their breath and time? They are being used to keep others in jobs. They need to take ownership of their minds and not be the puppets of others. The panel are only there to score personal points and are really not interested in what the audience has to say.

Did you know that during the run up to a general election our attention gets focused on four main issues, Health, Education, Defence and Crime? They seem to debate these four issues all the time anyway. These issues are distractions that elections are won or lost on. These four issues are the agenda for the electorate to hold debates about, but what are the hidden agendas that the politicians keep quiet about?

Don't you find it incredible that just a few hundred people decide how some sixty million other people live? How can that be right? Surely such a system is in need of radical change. The main political parties have passed the same system to each other for far too long. We have heard the same old stuff for far too long. We have been ripped off for far too long.

The electorate do not elect a Prime Minister or members of the cabinet. They also do not elect anyone into other positions of power. Yet the people sit back and allow themselves to be ripped off and abused by these so-called trusted servants.

Why do people who vote a Government into power often take to the streets in protest when that government imposes restrictions or hardships on them? Why did they bother to vote in the first place? Do remember that when the next election comes around one choice open to you is not to vote for anyone.

You really do not have to vote. People have been so indoctrinated into voting that they think they have to vote for someone. Don't continue to give politicians permission to restrict your life. Another word for addiction is dependency and most people have been duped into being dependent on governments to look after them.

Did you know that 93% of people responding to a poll agreed that politicians were paid too much? If you think that, why vote for them? Disclosures have shown that politicians are claiming millions of £££s in expenses and yet people they are suppose to be representing are living on the poverty line.

When government wants to bring in laws to control us more, they feed us the line that the new laws will crack down on organised crime, terrorism and fraud. These claims are complete testicles. To those who object they say, "If you have nothing to hide then you have nothing to fear". This is just another form of testicles used to gag people. Many people know who the real frauds are.

At this time of writing there are moves to introduce identity cards. This will almost be the ultimate in control. We already have birth certificates, NHS numbers, national insurance numbers, passports, credit/debit cards, bank accounts, loyalty reward cards, surveys, motor insurance, car road tax, driving licences, TV licences, electoral registers, Inland Revenue, credit reference agencies, population census, CCTV, council tax, vehicle registration, utility bills, mobile phones, home computers… How many more ways do they need to tag us and keep us under surveillance? If they are allowed to get away with introducing Identity cards, what will be next?

Maybe their next move will be to get rid of cash. Just think, everything you bought, even a newspaper, would be paid for with a "smart card". They have been slowly working away at this for several years. The latest moves have been to get the elderly to have their pensions paid into bank accounts and the reluctance to join the Euro currency system. The "smart card" is already in the waiting room. Could such moves be because they now realise that, like Christian religion, they are losing their grip on the people? Let's face it many people no longer vote at elections. Why do you suppose that is? Desperate measures like postal voting, internet voting and proposals to lower the age of voting to sixteen suggests that government is concerned about its future.

The Royal Family and the Honours List and both Houses of Parliament have all become objects of ridicule and a laughing-stock. I wouldn't want the Royal Family living next door to me. Britain is not GREAT; the GREAT has been exposed as a placebo. Much of Britain is overdosing on testicles. They now use the word "SPIN" which is a four letter spelling of testicles.

There seems to be a never ending stream of focus groups, feasibility studies, meetings, committee meetings, subcommittee meetings, glossy brochures, bulletins, newsletters, speeches and "Your Questions Answered". This one is real prize testicles. They come up with a list of their own questions and then supply the answers to them. All of these things can be used as placebos, by those in authority, to dupe the public into believing that great and wonderful things are being done. It is quite often activity instead of action.

DON'T SWALLOW THE TESTICLES

Signs of social and civil unrest are emerging and the day may come when the prevailing system could come to an end. The likely time for this to take place would be during the 2020 – 2030 decade, though it could happen before. The babies of the sixties are going to be retiring in their masses during that decade and experiencing financial, medical and social deprivation. They and their feral descendants could bring about a collapse of the status quo. Large numbers are already demonstrating what is to come. The present government is desperately trying to mend the many holes that are appearing in the fabric that has been woven over many years but it is all coming apart and slipping away from their grasp.

Many of the present younger generation are not frightened of authority. Many of them regard an Anti Social Behaviour Order (ASBO) as a status symbol that adds weight to their street CV.

Sometime ago Prime Ministers questions were changed from the afternoon to the mornings (PM to AM). Was anyone surprised? The liquid lunches that were being consumed were becoming far too evident during the afternoon sessions. Do you ever watch that load of testicles? These are the people who are running the country! Better behaviour can be seen at most football grounds.

What about the present Prime Minister? Americans have told me that he is the best Vice President they've ever had. Have you seen the American style press meetings that he now holds? What a load of testicles. When was the last time you heard him mention "cabinet decision"? This Prime Minister is heading a neo conservative quartet style of government and everyone else does as they are told.

Last year he had his master, Mr. President, over from America for a visit. It is said to have cost the taxpayers of this country five million pounds. The only glimpse most people saw of Mr. President was of him being driven around the grounds of Buckingham Palace.

Did you watch the run up to the presidential election in the USA? Millions of sheep people there attended rallies wearing stupid hats and waving banners and flags to show their support for one of two men who both wanted exactly the same thing, POWER. It became so obvious that they were both prepared to say anything to get votes. They were desperately trying to please all of the people. The political parties here in the UK are now trying to steer us through a similar process of testicles.

Mr. President was returned to office. Millions of Americans voted for the killing of their own soldiers and other innocent people to continue and for the kidnapping and incarceration of innocent people to continue as well. Where is it going to end? They talk about peace and yet continue killing.

Now Mr. President has his gaze fixed on Iran. Taking over Iraq will give him a good base to launch an invasion from. Can he take over the Middle East in the four years that he has as President or will we see another member of his family follow him into the White House to carry on the family business?

There is now doubt as to the existence of a terrorist organisation that the world was told is called Al Qaeda. Why has the most wanted man in the world not been caught? The great shows that are presented to us through the media here in the UK of troops guarding airports and mock germ warfare exercises are no more than carefully orchestrated pieces of scaremongering to make us think that we are in danger and that the government is doing all that it can to try to protect us.

DON'T SWALLOW THE TESTICLES

The Prime Minister saw Mr. President returned to the White House on the terrorism ticket and he probably thinks that he can get returned to Downing Street on the same ticket.

Let us hope that Mr. President's pupil is not returned to power in the UK at the next general election. These two minds seem to have merged into one arrogant destructive force. The pupil was ready and the teacher appeared. The pupil has even copied his master's swagger. These two are self-confessed Christians (I'd rather take my chances with the lions). I always thought that a Christian was someone who followed the teachings of Christ, but I guess that if you want votes bad enough you will claim to be anything. Perhaps, like many Christians, they know the psalm but not the shepherd.

The bible says that God created all animals and gave man dominion over them and yet this Prime Minister has banned fox hunting. It just goes to show that politics can be for those who believe in God and for those who don't believe in God and for those who think they are God.

At this moment in time the government has announced that it is going to axe jobs in the civil service and the armed forces. They have informed the public that these cuts will make savings of millions of pounds. What they haven't said is how much it is going to cost to keep all of these people out of work.

The government's production line starts when we are born. The child's birth is registered and they are issued with a National Health Service number. The next step is to put the child through the education system.

There is play school and pre-school before actual school itself. The child passes through the education system being fed testicles all the way.

DON'T SWALLOW THE TESTICLES

Schools are concerned with their own image and reaching targets and where they feature in the school league tables and pandering to Ofsted Inspectors. The pupil is just a pawn in a much bigger game that is being played out by others. One way or another we are all caught up in other people's games whether we be NHS patients, the disabled, the elderly, the abused, the unemployed, customers; all can be pawns caught up in the games of others.

For years children have been sent to school and told that if they do well and get good marks then when they leave school they will get a good job with a good company. What a load of testicles. Good teachers, like a good parent, should constantly strive to do themselves out of a job. Often a school report tells more about the teacher than about the pupil. Allow children to grow wings, instil in them an entrepreneurial spirit, let them have ownership of their minds and when they leave school they will soar. Why should it matter whether or not they are a credit to the school?

Letting the young stay on at school until they are eighteen and making it easier for them to pass exams and go on to university is a good way of keeping thousands of people off the unemployment register for six-year periods.

These days there is no need for someone to spend four years of their life at university or amass the huge debt that goes with it. If their ambition is to be financially independent then there are opportunities that can help them achieve it within those four years. Yes, their parents will be deprived of a photograph, to put on the cabinet, of their child wearing a mortarboard and gown.

The education system is designed to lead pupils towards the governments forty five year PAYE plan:

- Poverty
- As
- You
- Earn

This plan will ensure that they join the job mind-set and once in it they will remain in it because they will become addicted to that monthly pay cheque. Their only way out of this trap will be if they wake up and realise that there are other ways to make a living. Not many people wake up and take a real hard look at the daily drudgery of their lives and decide to change it. Most people trek their way through the forty five year plan that had been passed down to them and at the end of it discover the other meaning of PAYE:

- Poverty
- After
- You've
- Earned

They now join the weekly post office queue and buy two telephone stamps, charge a meter key with £5 of electricity and look around supermarkets for items of food with "reduced price" stickers on them. What way is that to live for twenty or more years? What else can they do though on a state pension?

Do you know of anyone who made the decision when they left school that they would retire broke? So where did they go wrong? What will you have when you retire? Do you know how much tax is being taken from you? Let's take a look.

- National Insurance is a tax
- Income Tax
- V.A.T. on most things you buy
- Car Road Tax
- Duty paid on goods that you buy and bring back from your holiday
- Council Tax
- Parking Meters is a tax
- Car Park charges are a tax
- Car Parking Permits are a tax
- Fines imposed on you are a tax
- Bridge and Tunnel Tolls are a tax
- Road Congestion charges are a tax

Do you see how your earnings are being taxed over and over again? Is it any wonder that people are retiring after forty or fifty years of work with fuck all to show for it? The Governments that you keep voting for are taking most of your money from you. How much longer are you going to allow them to do this?

If you are caught up in the governments forty five year plan and want to get out of it then take action NOW that will bring about a change. If you fail to address your situation you will be in that post office queue before you know it, then you will become a member of the TIOC, The If Only Club.

Politics is a deceptive business. One attribute that makes a good politician is the ability to speak testicles fluently. Many politicians possess that attribute. Perhaps a more apt name for The Houses of Parliament would be The Scrotum.

I don't believe a word that any politician says and I don't vote in elections. Why is this? It's because I refuse to be assigned a role in their game of testicles. You make your own choice.

DON'T SWALLOW THE TESTICLES

I am not patriotic and I enjoy watching national and international sports because I can appreciate the talents of all players and all countries and it really doesn't matter to me what side wins because I am not supporting any of them.

I would not allow myself to dress in a uniform and be sent to fight people who have done me no harm. I don't see the people who decided to invade Iraq out there fighting alongside the troops. Let those who start conflicts do their own fighting. Patriotism and altruism are testicles used to goad people into doing things that others have initiated. Take ownership of your mind and don't allow yourself to be wrapped in a flag and fed the testicles of anthems to sing-a-long to as you charge headlong into the games of others.

4
Here is Your Daily Dose of Fear

"Good evening and welcome to the news at ..." "Today's top story is ..." Whose news and whose top/lead story is it? What we are given is the news that the programme makers have decided they want us to have and that becomes the issues that most people get locked into.

Have you noticed that much of this so-called news is fear based? Why do you suppose that is? If you were presented with a frightening story that you had been given to believe could affect you personally then surely it's in your interest to keep following that story, which means you watching the news and reading the newspapers. This is the carefully laid trap that you have walked into and before this one has blown over there is another one already being laid. It's rather like getting two bells on the winning line on a gaming machine; you just have to put another coin in. Or the cliff-hanger ending to an episode of one of those soaps, you just have to watch the next one.

The media play both villain and hero in presenting their news. In the role of villain they lay the fear trap for the susceptible. Then they play the hero by giving updates on the scare story, with reassurances that the situation is under control and the world has not ended. The susceptible have been rescued from the big bad dragon.

Last year there was a change in the way that television news

DON'T SWALLOW THE TESTICLES

programmes are presented. News presenters now spend the first half standing up to tell us the so-called news and the second half sitting down. The new layout resembles a catwalk and was probably designed for the Prima Donna presenters among them to prance up and down. These changes were announced as giving their news "a new look". This can translate as meaning putting a new cover on an old book. It certainly hasn't made a difference to the testicles that they call news.

Why is it that the media can't just report what's happening? What's wrong with saying, "Firemen are on strike in Salford"? Why do they have to embroider it with testicles? "The public are being put at risk". "Schools may have to close because of the potential risks to children". "Elderly live in fear of fire at nursing home". They interview one poor old soul who says, "It's frightening to think what could happen". They don't report that all the other residents are not frightened. They love to use children and the elderly because it's emotive and can stir up so-called public reaction which in turn keeps a story on the boil.

The media, more often than not, grope in the dark with half stories, innuendo and surmise in their attempts to acquire the actual facts surrounding a story. They also need to run with the hares as well as with the hounds. Do you think those reporters who travel with the Prime Minister would get a seat on the plane if they were anti PM or couldn't be relied on when needed? Do remember that you do not have to speak to reporters. You have a right to remain silent. They may print all kinds of things in the hope that you will fill in the gaps but don't supply them with information that could do you harm.

If you get yourself in the media spotlight then you run the risk of someone from your past popping up to tell the nation what an utter shit you were to them.

DON'T SWALLOW THE TESTICLES

The media have become the self elected conscience of society. They have set themselves up as an unelected political force that can influence those who watch, read or listen to them. They have even taken over the role of Christian religion as Purveyors of Misery and hopefully they will go the same way as Christian religion.

Take a look through most magazines and daily newspapers, listen to radio or TV news programmes and you will read or hear about breast cancer, lung cancer, skin cancer, prostate cancer, heart disease, diabetes, asthma, high cholesterol, obesity, arthritis, strokes, stress and any other so-called crisis that they can come up with. They bombard us every day with these so-called health concerns. It's testicles. No wonder doctor's waiting rooms are full of people, many of them who think they are ill. The cause is probably autosuggestion brought on by reading testicles in newspapers, magazines and listening to what is said on radio and TV.

Have you watched those early morning breakfast programmes? They seem to be made up mostly of five minute topic slots. If you want to confirm what I have said then just record a whole week of these programmes and then play them back when you have some time to spare. You will be amazed at how many people will get up in the small hours to go on television for a couple of minutes to speak some old testicles.

One of the recent Saturday tabloid papers contained one hundred pages! How did they manage to find such a vast amount of testicles to write about? What about those weekend papers that have half a dozen or more supplements of additional testicles inside of them? They should have a Testicle Writer of the Year Award; I would imagine that there would be a mass of nominations.

DON'T SWALLOW THE TESTICLES

Just a few months ago there were thousands of people dying the most awful deaths around the world and yet one tabloid paper gave its whole front page to a footballer who had learnt a few words of Spanish. He should try learning English first. It is another example of just how much the publicity junkies are running the media mental asylum.

There was a programme on TV recently about the Paparazzi and one guy reckons he got over £100,000 from a newspaper for a set of photographs of a female publicity junkie who was exercising on a beach wearing a bikini. How can photographs of her be worth that much? Could it be that she doesn't shit, piss and fart like everyone else?

Many newspapers are obsessed with these publicity junkies. I couldn't give a fuck who these people are seen with or whose home they are seen leaving in the early hours of the morning or what they wear. These shallow people seem to be consumed with themselves and most of what they have to say tends to lack depth and weight. This characteristic would make them good politicians.

Did you know that there are annual awards for journalists/reporters? One is for the reporter of the year. These are events where they all get together and clap each other. Who wins these awards? Have you seen those reporters who stand in water up to their waist and tell us about floods in that area? Then there are those reporters who get themselves blown along sea fronts and at the same time try to tell us about the storm force gales. Could that be the sort of testicles that puts them in the running for an award?

During the past year we have witnessed what the force of nature is capable of. One of the things I find quite remarkable is that in the midst of serious flooding there are people whose instant response seems to be to grab a camera or camcorder and take pictures of the event. These people probably see themselves as budding Paparazzi. I think that my own instant response would be to get as far away and as quickly as I could. One image that conjured up in my mind was of some poor bastard floating down the road clinging to the roof of his house and some wanker with a camera shouts out to him, "Say cheese"!

Presenters at these award functions have been known to state that, "Reporters risk their lives to bring news from around the world to the British people". Who asked them to? Did you? If reporters are risking their lives for a story or an award then maybe they should reflect on that. Surely there is enough going on in this country for them to report, or perhaps it makes this country look better by reporting what goes on elsewhere.

Have you noticed that when there is a lull in murder and mayhem, we then get told that recent research has found that something or other that we eat or drink or use is killing thousands of us each year? Isn't that just so comforting to know? Have you ever heard them announce that recent research has found something that does us an absolute power of good? Where do the media get all these research reports from? Research is always inconclusive. Don't take too much notice of it. Like many other things it is based on the tried and tested and proven theory that testicles baffle brains.

Where do the programme makers find all those so-called experts, specialists, psychologists, analysts, nutritionists, dieticians, therapists, economists, statisticians, etc, that they call in to support the testicles that the news presenters have been given to dish out to the susceptible? Having a degree in psychology doesn't mean that someone is a psychologist. Who checks the credentials of these so-called experts? How many of these so-called experts are licenced to practice? Recently I heard one of them remark, "The country is in crisis". It was benevolent of him to make such a sweeping statement on behalf of us all. If these experts are being used to influence people then it's only right and proper that their credentials be made known to those people, but it would be so much better if we could be saved from the experts of the world. It seems that the more experts we have the more problems we have.

If ever you are told that research has discovered something, whether it's good or bad, don't believe it until you have satisfied yourself on the following four counts.

- Who funded it?
- Who commissioned it?
- What were the terms of reference?
- What are the results to be used for?

Why don't the news programme makers ask these four questions to those who announce findings of research? Could it be because they would rather leave the viewers believing that something could harm them? More fear tactics.

Research can produce different results for the same thing. It depends on what the terms of reference are by those funding the research. One company might want to sell a product that they claim is good for you and so they commission research to test the product and produce evidence to support their claim. A rival company wanting to discredit those findings may have research carried out in order to show that certain ingredients in the product are not good for you. At the end of the day who are you to believe? Those who commission research are not necessarily the ones who are funding it.

DON'T SWALLOW THE TESTICLES

Now let's look at this bogeyman called fear. Fear exists in the mind and is caused by accepting the negative. I'm sure that people in Iraq have plenty of cause to be fearful at this moment in time. The fear that I want to talk about is the fear that is created by the use of propaganda/testicles. Today we hear terms like, "The fear of crime". "People are living in fear". Where does this sort of stuff come from?

One technique that is often used by the police and security companies to get public opinion on crime is a questionnaire. The questionnaire is sent out to selected households and the questions tend to be closed and only require yes or no answers or a tick in a box. The chosen ones, being dutiful citizens, return the completed questionnaires and somehow or other the answers reveal that 85% of people are living in fear of crime. What a lot of testicles.

The media tend to use "The money making phone-in poll" technique. The viewers/readers are asked to phone one number if they agree with a selected item of testicles that is in the news or another number if they disagree with it, or they can text using another number. Then they are told "Don't worry if you can't get through, the lines are open until midnight. If the lines are busy keep trying, we will bring you the results tomorrow". They never disclose how many people phoned in; they give the results in percentages because they sound more impressive. You don't need many people to phone in to calculate percentages. Three people are 75% of four people.

Don't allow yourself to be used in this way. These industries strive to make people dependent on them. They want you to watch their news programmes, read their newspapers and buy burglar alarms, CCTV, panic alarms and anything else that will make you a prisoner in your own home. These people don't deal in security they deal in insecurity and they have been the main contributors towards the creation of it. The old adage that if you want to sell something to someone then you must first convince them that they need it still holds true.

When you next hear these scare stories on TV news or read them in the newspapers just remember the following antidote for fear.

- False
- Evidence
- Appears
- Real

They want you to think that it means.

- Fuck
- Everything
- And
- Run

Take ownership of your mind and see all this media stuff for what it really is, just another industry using whatever methods it can to make money from selling its commodity to susceptible people.

5
Don't Prosecute Yourself

Television news programmes often show police smashing their way through the front door of someone's house and once inside doing what they like to the rest of the home. The public are told that this was a drugs raid that had been planned for months. Some cannabis is found in the house, those arrested are later released without charge and the operation involved twenty officers. Who gave the police permission to engage in this kind of costly so-called reality TV entertainment? Whilst this carefully orchestrated load of testicles might look good for them it isn't what the police should be engaged in.

Did you watch that TV programme last year called "Rail Cops"? It was about the British Transport Police. There were two particular mouthy old bags in it that seemed to have got carried away with being on TV.

There was another programme of testicles called "MacIntyre's Big Sting". They went to elaborate lengths to arrest petty criminals for the non payment of fines and other minor offences. They should have been able to pick these guys up on the streets but they failed to do so. They took these people into custody from the show and released most of them again within hours. Why didn't they arrest them as soon as they arrived at the venue? Why make a television programme about it? They seem to have plenty of funds and police officers available to engage in these pathetic actions.

DON'T SWALLOW THE TESTICLES

The police seem to be obsessed with publicity and how they are perceived. Whenever there is a murder they quickly get the relatives of the victim to go on television to make an appeal. On the rare occasions that they claim to make a coup they entertain the public with another carefully orchestrated piece of work by providing armed convoys, to ferry those arrested, to and from court. This can plant the idea in the minds of the public that the people that have been arrested must be bad if the police are taking all these precautions.

Why do the police take TV camera crews with them on so-called drug raids and onto the streets to film them doing the job that they are paid to do? How do TV companies obtain copies of taped interviews between police and suspects and copies of CCTV footage from inside of police stations? How do TV camera crews and reporters know what time an accused person is going to be transported from a police station to the local court? They obviously obtain this information from somewhere and surely there can only be one original source but no one seems to ask questions about these matters.

We have a police force in this country that has been given far too much power and we are in danger of becoming a police state. Have you seen the amount of gear police officers carry around on them? It's a wonder they can move.

Why do they need all this gear anyway? Much of their job today involves them delegating their work onto the public. Somewhere along the line they discovered that it's a lot easier to get the public to do your job than to do it yourself. Doing this gives them a good cop out (pun intended) for not solving crime because they can blame the public for not helping them.

Two instances of the delegation of their work are

"Crimestoppers" and "Crimewatch UK". Employing these methods make the police look incompetent. They have had millions of pounds of resources poured into them and yet they seem to know very little about crime and criminal detection. They, like Benefit Fraud, want the public to do their work for them by becoming informers.

We appear to have a police force that is more concerned with its image than with detecting crime.

If you should find yourself involved with the police, regarding allegations of a criminal nature, do exercise your fundamental right to remain silent. If a police officer asks you to accompany him to a police station, decline the offer. He will then have two options. He can remove himself from your presence or he can arrest you. If you volunteer to go to a police station to help the police with their inquiries then you may find that until you are actually arrested they don't have to inform you of your rights.

If you are arrested by a police officer he must, at the earliest opportunity, caution you and make it known to you that you are not obliged to say anything. That means you do not have to say anything. If you are arrested you will probably be taken to a police station where you will be made aware of PACE, the Police and Criminal Evidence Act.

This act, by its very name, presumes you to be a criminal. You have been taken to a police station on so-called suspicion of having committed an offence; you have not been convicted and are therefore not a criminal. Do not allow the police to take away your power. You do not have to go into an interview room and answer questions that will be recorded. The police always control interviews because they are the ones asking the

DON'T SWALLOW THE TESTICLES

questions. Don't sit in an interview room and say, "no comment" (you are in fact making a comment) to every question that is put to you; it can be made to sound bad if you end up in court. If you are appointed a duty solicitor or if you have your own one, instruct him/her to inform the police to either charge you or release you.

If you are arrested you say nothing. If an attempt is made, at any time, to question you further you say nothing. Remain calm and in possession of your mind at all times. You will probably be locked in a cell and have your personal effects taken from you. You should question the legality of these actions. Do not sign for your personal effects at the time they are taken from you or when they are returned to you. If the police inform you that they are going to release you on police bail tell them that you don't wish to be released on police bail. Do not sign the bail form. You have not been charged with a criminal offence, so why would you want to sign a bail form? Do not report back to the police station on the date they ask you to. Make sure that you obtain the names of everyone involved in your arrest and detention.

If a police officer arrests you and you are detained and later released without being charged then you can make a claim against that officer for wrongful arrest and unlawful detention. Don't be fobbed off with the testicles that you can only make a claim against the constabulary. Police officers should ensure that they have adequate insurance to cover themselves in the event of a claim being made against them.

Remember, if you plead not guilty to a charge and your case is sent to trial it is for twelve people to decide if you are guilty or not.

DON'T SWALLOW THE TESTICLES

What about the testicles they dish out to us that they call annual crime figures? Once again they use statistics, or lies as one past politician called them. They say things like there has been a 10% drop in violent crime but opportunity crime has risen by 15%. How do we know if we are being told the truth, the whole truth and nothing but the truth? Chief Constables, like politicians, are skilled in the art of fancy verbal footwork. They never miss an opportunity to get more resources from government to fight a particular type of crime or police an event or protect the population from the latest threat from terrorism. What a growth industry they've created.

It's a good idea to learn some law. You don't need to become a solicitor, but with the way things are these days knowing something about the law could stand you in good stead. Familiarise yourself with The Human Rights Act, The Police and Criminal Evidence Act, The Road Traffic Act and laws on Employment, Family, Property and anything else that you consider would be of use to you. Find a good book on basic law and spend thirty minutes a day, every day, reading it along with this book.

I know that I sound a bit hard on "The Blue Line" but I actually believe that the police do a thankless job. I do not believe that we need more police officers. I believe that police officers should be used more efficiently and more effectively and that they should have the handcuffs removed that government has placed on them.

6
Testicles Won't Make You Look Younger

Why can't there be a weekly A - Z published that lists all new products that are coming out during that week? It could include a brief description about the product and its uses. This would inform us about new products and leave us to make our own minds up about them.

That, of course, is not going to happen. Companies go to great lengths and great expense (reflected in the inflated price of the products) to tell us how great and wonderful their products are and how we couldn't possibly live without them.

Many companies now use so-called celebrities in advertising campaigns. Why is that? Would you buy a product just because a so-called celebrity was paid to endorse it? How do you know if this nonentity actually uses the product? Do you think this so-called celebrity was chosen because the company heard that he/she was already using the product? Let's be candid, if someone doesn't use it, eat it, drink it, wear it, sleep in it, drive it, own it, shop in it, live in it, have it, or holiday at it, then they shouldn't be endorsing it.

There was an advert on TV last year about settees and sofas with one of those so-called celebrities being paid to say "I like them I think you will to". Saying she likes them and saying she has one are two entirely different things. People who go out and buy these settees and sofas are going to be paying over the top for the eight words uttered by this person.

Recently I saw a poster of a rugby player advertising "After Shave Lotion". He had about a week of stubble on his face. I rechecked, it definitely said "After Shave".

These publicity junkies are also used to encourage us to get into debt, to part with our blood and to get us to part with yet more of our money by giving it to charities. Who told these people that they are celebrities anyway? I would like to see a TV programme produced called, If You're a Celebrity Get the Fuck Out of Here. I would vote with both hands.

My dictionary defines "Celebrity" as "a well-known person". How many celebrities are personally well known to you? Celebrities are not well known, they are known about. There is a big difference between knowing someone and knowing about someone. You can only know another person if that person chooses to reveal to you who they really are, not what they are. I have to say that I haven't a clue who these people are who appear on television and in newspapers and are referred to as celebrities.

Do you ever get the feeling that some of these so-called celebrities, or publicity junkies as I prefer to call them, would live in the sewer if it meant them getting media attention? Do you believe that these people are successful? How do you measure success? Don't confuse success with fame.

Most of these people are like little boys and girls whistling in the dark to comfort themselves. Deep down inside they know that their use by date is quite short and that the moment they drop out of the media spotlight they are finished. The next time that you are in a shop, that sells newspapers and magazines take a look at the front cover of most of the magazines, there will probably be one or more of these so-called celebrities telling about some hellish event that happened to them at some time or other. They seem to be so fearful of not being in the media spotlight anymore.

Some of these publicity junkies are now having their own brands of perfume produced. I expect a tennis player could call their brand Service! A snooker player might call their brand Balls! A footballer might call their brand Score! Just imagine if you saw a bottle in the store that said Score from VD!

The media created the celebrity culture and turned it into a big money making industry and the media decide who is in and who is out. When someone outlives their usefulness they are thrown on the scrap heap.

The real stars are those who don't have to prove anything. These guys tend to live in Los Angeles and other such places and have no need of publicity. In the United Kingdom we have only a very small number of stars and far too many publicity junkies who think they are stars.

Don't you get just a little pissed off with the testicles that are used to advertise products on TV? Why have women, after years of struggle for equality and independence, allowed themselves to be used to con each other? One reason could be that women have been targeted by many industries as being gullible and susceptible.

Many times, when I see certain adverts with women in who are being paid to dupe other women into buying products that is claimed will make them look younger, slimmer, and healthier I find myself thinking, "How fucking pathetic". Don't get heated about my comment ladies, I get the same thought when I see men doing the same to other men.

Do you really believe that something you wash your hair with will give it more bounce and more shine? What do you think that is on the top of your head, a polished tennis ball? Do you also believe that a cream that you apply to your face will do all kinds of wonderful things to your skin while you sleep? How will you know, if you are asleep? If there was a cream that vanished wrinkles most people wouldn't be able to afford to buy it.

What is that blue colour liquid that they pour onto those panty liners in that advert? Is it a discharge from the "bladder weakness" that they refer to? Quite a few of those adverts have educated men about women. So ladies beware! If you invite a man back to your place "for coffee" the first thing he is likely to do is ask to use the bathroom and once there he is going to look in the cabinet for thrush treatment cream, diarrhoea or constipation tablets, bladder weakness pads and other tell tale products that might give him a clue to what he might be letting himself in for. If he finds any he is going to forgo the coffee and be legging it down the road fast.

Many men probably think that women go to bed at night with lotion on their hair, cream on their faces, eye pads on and a gum shield in their mouths to whiten their teeth. They don't need to announce that they have a headache anymore.

Don't allow yourself to be duped into buying products that you see advertised. We are bombarded with products today, all of them telling us how great they will make us look and feel. Things are not always what they appear to be. Very careful thought goes into marketing a product and some adverts are so well done you can almost taste or feel the product.

DON'T SWALLOW THE TESTICLES

When you see an advert for shampoo, cosmetics and other such things, picture in your mind what you don't see; the lighting and special effects, the man with the clapperboard and the cameras. Look closely at the person being used in the ad, how old is he/she? Advertising is designed to attack your self-image and to undermine you. It suggests to you that you can't be alright unless you use this particular product, wear these clothes, drink this stuff, holiday at this destination, and drive this type of car. The testicles of marketing psychology are everywhere. Don't let up on your resolve to keep ownership of your mind in all matters. Remember, unless you stand for something you will fall for anything.

I once heard some clown describe himself as "a celebrity hair colourist". So what, who gives a toss? The other day a car passed me and sign written on the car was "Cosmetic Nail Technician", what a load of testicles. Take a look in the Classified Phone Books and see how many people claim to be a "specialist".

If you see any of the following sales testicles on products, avoid them like the plague. "Incredible Results", "Look Fabulous", "Look and Feel Fantastic", "You Will Be Amazed" "Look Ten Years Younger", "Lose Pounds", (they probably mean ££££s).

The next time that you are in a chemist shop, take a look at the different brands of toothpaste. They don't seem to care about whether or not they clean your teeth the emphasis is on how white your teeth will look. The ones that claim to make your teeth whiter than all the others will cost you more than all the others. Someone commented to me that one particular brand tasted like "pigeon shit", I didn't ask him how he knew. One brand that I noticed claimed to "Revitalise, Whiten,

Remineralise, Tone Gums and contain Energising Mint". What the fuck does all that mean? Take a look too at all the facial lotions and creams, they all make claims about how good they will make you look. Which one will you allow yourself to be conned into buying?

The only people who need many of these products are the people who make them. Years ago the public were told that a certain chocolate bar a day would help them "work, rest and play". What a load of testicles. Today companies use similar words by telling us that their products will make us look good and feel good all day long. Testicles!

If you feel good about yourself then you will look good and that feeling will last forever. The testicles of marketing psychology want you to believe that if you look good you will feel good. Just because a house has a beautiful garden doesn't mean that everything is alright inside the house. You can only look good for a certain length of time and then you are going to have to do something to make you look good again. You are going to age, you are going to lose your hair or turn grey, you are going to get wrinkles and your arse is probably going to travel south. What is it going to matter if you can pass for seventy when you are eighty? If you keep putting all that crap on your face you might pass for eighty when you are fifty.

The only question you ever need to ask yourself when considering buying something is what are the benefits and advantages to me if I buy this thing? If someone is trying to sell you something then the only question you ever need to ask them is what are the benefits and advantages to you if I buy this thing? Isn't life simple?

7
Unreality Television

Most of the main television channels are almost a never-ending stream of so-called Make Overs, Gardening, Cooking and TV Reality programmes. Throw in with that lot, the soaps and other fodder and that is the so-called viewing for the week, every week. There is no need to buy a TV Guide each week; the one that you bought at the start of the year will give you a good idea of all the testicles that is going to be on throughout the year.

At this time of writing this there is a nightly TV reality programme on. In it is a mixture of so-called celebrities (yes, more of them). The aim is to find which one is the best chef. The only real Cook amongst them dropped out on the first day. In charge is a devil of a chef who makes his presence felt by fucking swearing at almost everyone working in the kitchen, the headwaiter and some of the customers. The customers just happen to be more so-called celebrities. Stars wouldn't be seen dead in the place.

The programme appears to be directed from behind the scenes with instructions being relayed through an earpiece to the chef in charge. One has to consider the possibility that he is being told who to swear at and who to wind up. These guys are slowly being whittled down from ten to one by a viewer's phone-in voting system and the one left will be the winner.

It is very noticeable that the number of votes that each person receives is not made known to the viewers and that is suspect. This programme may not be looking for the person who is the best chef but for the one who can keep the viewing public phoning in. Why can't we be shown the interviews, discussions, contracts and the programme planning that took place during the run up to the programme itself? That would make a programme that was much more enlightening, entertaining and interesting.

On one of the other channels another series of big something or other (I can't bring myself to say the name) has started. BIG TESTICLES would be a more apt name for it. BIG, BIG TESTICLES would describe it even better. Where did they find this bunch of devious sad misfits that they call housemates? They look like they were taken out of one of those treatment centres. Millions of people will watch this load of testicles over the coming weeks and it will probably be one of their main talking points during that time. If you were to offer these people an opportunity that could increase their income and improve their life style many of them would tell you that they don't have the time. Do you see how people are intoxicated by these TV programmes? They will waste hours of their lives watching this mindless junk but they won't do anything that will improve their own lives.

Would you visit a local factory and ask if you could spend an hour each day watching the employees at work, then at the end of the hour phone the manager and tell him which one of his work force you think he should get rid of? What would you say to someone who did that?

Wake up! Take ownership of your mind. Why do you think I keep saying those words? Don't be a TV show pawn phoning in with your vote. These shows are unreal until the viewer makes them real by inviting them into their lives. Television is an influential magician that creates illusions. Things are not always what they appear to be. Think about the reality of your own life. Would you like to change it?

Have you noticed that most of these so-called reality shows are on TV channels that show commercials between breaks? Why do you suppose that is? These commercials generate revenue for the TV companies. If a business wants their product advertised during prime time then it will cost them more than if it was advertised during the morning or afternoon. If a business wants their product advertised during a programme that is watched by millions of people then it will cost even more for the simple reason that it is going to reach more people.

TV companies, like all other businesses, are first and foremost financially driven. They are therefore going to create money making masquerades that are likely to draw millions of viewers to them. Every programme is a gamble for them. Watch the type of advert that is shown during a popular TV show. Count how many commercial breaks there are and how many adverts are shown during those breaks. On those shows that have phone-in voting, why don't they inform the viewers what the total votes are for each contestant? On those shows that say 16p, or whatever, from every call will be donated to charity, why don't they say how much was sent and which charities it was given to? Could it be because they don't want the viewing public to know how much profit they have made from all the calls? Yes they do get BIG revenue from all those calls. Or could it be because the votes don't really matter. Why do the presenters on these shows say during voting "it's neck and neck" or "it's too close to call at present"? It's because they want people to keep phoning in. The shows are all about making money, nothing else.

Now are you beginning to see why I said, "Don't be a TV pawn phoning in with your vote". You are being used as a source of revenue. Why not cut back on the TV and start creating a source of revenue for yourself?

These so-called TV reality shows are probably going to be produced more and more because of the vast amount of money they make for the TV companies. The sad sheep people love and encourage them. They sit at home talking or perhaps shouting at the television set and telling it who they are or are not going to vote for. Some will even phone their friends to find out who they are going to vote for. This will mean even more revenue, for the telephone companies, from these shows. The sheep people obviously don't mind spending their money to help big businesses get richer.

Have you also noticed that many TV shows feature the same so-called celebrities? They keep appearing on quiz shows, reality shows, talk shows, dance shows and some even become pious on Sundays and tell us what their favourite hymns are.

They then create shows for themselves where they get awards for all the testicles they have contributed to the watching public. Then to cap it all they hold live audiences for each other. These are nice and safe events for them and no one will be attacked. No prizes for guessing who makes up the audience. When there is a welcome break in these programmes we are treated to a showing of more so-called celebrities in the adverts.

Another series of Celebrity Big Testicles has just finished. Not wanting to be accused of contempt prior to investigation I watched it for two evenings. I had only heard of two of the

DON'T SWALLOW THE TESTICLES

so-called housemates. The whole thing was designed to make money. Some of the nation's intelligent levels are obviously sinking fast if they are allowing themselves to be fobbed off with this load of testicles that a TV company has served up as entertainment.

These so-called celebrities have monopolised the main TV channels and by doing so have caused those channels to become stale. Some of these people can't even speak properly. Most of these people should be uprooted and sent packing and new people brought in to put some freshness and sanity back into TV. In my view there are only about half a dozen or so people that are adept at what they do and who continue to provide good quality TV entertainment.

Let me leave you with one final point about some of these shows. They seem to be more about generating income, presenters and judges than about contestants. The presenters and judges of these shows have advanced themselves and their careers and enlarged their CVs to a much greater level than any of the contestants. In fact most of the contestants from these shows just pale into obscurity after a short time.

8
What Are You Putting Into Your Body?

I've met many older people who have been swallowing prescribed medication for forty or more years and they have ended up with serious health problems in later life.

You should always ask your doctor what it is he/she is prescribing for you. Make them explain how they arrive at their diagnosis of you. Don't hand over your power to them. You need to know what you are taking into your body and what effect it could have on you. Have you any idea what forty years of pain killers, antibiotics, antidepressants, steroids, anti-inflammatorys and other conventional medication will do to you?

Have you seen the headache remedy medicines that say things like "Fast Acting", "Kills Pain Fast", "Instant Relief", and "Rapid Pain Relief"? You have probably noticed that most of these products contain the same ingredients. These products will cost you a lot more than just ordinary paracetamol and will do exactly the same job. Don't get taken in by the sales testicles, your headache will not go any quicker. When you see that sign that goes out around October each year and says, "It's That Flu Time Of Year" don't take too much notice of it. Keep ownership of your mind and the chances are you won't get headaches or flu.

Spend twenty minutes near the medicine counter at the chemist and see how many tablets and bottles of cough mixture they sell during that time. Go to the counter and ask if they have got anything for a headache and you will be sold something. You certainly won't be advised to go home and have a cup of tea and a rest. No wonder the pharmaceutical companies are such big business.

Have you noticed that there aren't many drugs available that can cure the illnesses of today but there seems to be no end of drugs for treating the symptoms of illnesses? Why is that?

Imagine that you are the head of a large pharmaceutical company with hundreds of share holders. Would you produce a drug that cured a disease and cost £100 or would you produce a drug that treated the symptoms of the disease and cost £1 per tablet and which someone took three or four times a day for the rest of their lives?

Cancer Research has been going for years and has failed to produce a cure for cancer and yet they continue to fund raise. Why, after all this time, have they not found a cure for cancer?

I'm a believer in eating wisely and there is just as much marketing psychology used about healthy eating and alternative medicine as there is about conventional medicine. You need to get the right information about the best products and companies.

I am in good all round health. I don't drink alcohol. I don't smoke. I sometimes have a decaffeinated coffee. I don't drink tea. I eat white bread. Every day I take the following:

- Vitamin E 400 I.U.
- Beta Carotene 15 mg Provitamin A
- Vitamin C 1000 mg

- Vitamin B Complex 500 mg
- High Strength Zinc 15 mg
- Omega 3 Fish Oil 1000 mg

If you had the car of your dreams wouldn't you look after it and put only the best oil and additives in it? Sure you would. You would want to get the best out of it and so it must be with our bodies. Don't put crap into your body, treat it with great respect and it will serve you well.

I don't jog or work out. I don't belong to sports clubs. I probably should walk more but the car usually seems to be the easier softer way.

Do the vitamins I take do me any good? I believe that they contribute to my all round good health. I once asked myself the question, "If millions of people around the world are taking vitamins and minerals every day where do the manufacturers keep getting all the ingredients from?"

When I was a kid we were told, "Eat your greens" and "An apple a day keeps the doctor away". What if those sayings are true? Judging by what we see today it doesn't look as if burgers, chips, crisps, chocolate, fizzy drinks and take-a-ways are doing many people much good.

Years ago there wasn't all this testicles about "sell by dates" and "use by dates". We didn't have fridge/freezers either. If you had some food left over you offered it to your neighbour. I can remember taking cheese and jam out of the larder and scraping mould off and eating them. I'm still here to tell the tale. People today throw away perfectly good food because it has a "use by" date on it. Don't take too much notice of all these so-called guidelines, someone somewhere is making money from them.

DON'T SWALLOW THE TESTICLES

Someone has recently claimed, "You are what you eat". Good sound advice from someone who has launched their own brand of health foods. What we think and believe matters much more because from these are formed our life principles and our actions. The main problems of man and woman are centred in their minds, or if you prefer, between their ears. Many people have a built in self destruct button, they tend to be their own worst enemy, their own judge and jury. When the self destruct button is pressed these people may carry out self inflicted punishment on themselves that can take the form of an attack being made on their body. Such an attack can take several forms and one form can be to stuff the body with crap food.

What about all the diet food that is around today? "Low Fat", "Skimmed", "Semi Skimmed", "Light", "Sugar Free" etc, etc. Then there are all the books and videos (usually done by so-called celebrities) and slimming clubs. What a huge industry has been created from the diet testicles. The more dieticians there are the more diets there are. The more nutritionists there are the more nutritional problems there are.

Let's go back to that Garden of Eden for a moment (mature view). We were told that God went looking for Adam and found him hiding. God said to him "Why are you hiding?" and Adam replied "Because I didn't want you to see me naked". God said to him "Who told you that you were naked?" Now I'm asking you; who told you that you are skinny, unattractive, no-good, from a dysfunctional family, have abandonment issues or any of the other testicles that you read or get told about today? Someone has been programming your mind and they have planted those seeds and you have allowed them to germinate. Don't stick other people's labels on yourself, that's why they're called "self-adhesive labels".

DON'T SWALLOW THE TESTICLES

Isn't it amazing how people fatten themselves up on crap food and then put themselves on diets or take themselves off to slimming clubs to try to get rid of the fat? Many people spend years and thousands of £££s on this merry go round. Stop cramming crap food into your mouth and you won't get fat. There really is no other way. You can control what goes into your mouth the same as you can control what comes out of it. Make a firm positive decision right now that you will stop eating crap food. If you go back on your decision later it will only mean one thing; you never really made a firm positive decision.

Don't give yourself an excuse why you can't do it, give yourself a reason why you can. How old are you going to be before you open the cage that you are in and set yourself free? Only you can do it because the handle is on the inside. You really can become the Managing Director of your own life. The oak tree sleeps inside the acorn. Take back and keep ownership of your mind. Make that firm positive decision to change and great things will happen.

9
Questionnaires, Surveys and Loyalty Reward Cards

Do you get sent those letters inviting you to apply for credit cards and loans? Often they are accompanied by an application form with most of your details already written in. Do you ever wonder how they got your details? Well, the chances are that somewhere along the line you filled in a questionnaire or a survey. It can easily happen. You get stopped in the street whilst out shopping, usually by a lady with a clip board and you are asked if you have a few minutes to spare to answer a few simple questions about some old testicles. You get thanked for your time and then you are asked for your name and address. Why? Because you have been so helpful they want to enter you in a free prize draw with the chance to win a holiday on some exotic island. Hopefully you give the details of someone you don't like and let them receive all the junk mail that is going to follow.

Have you ever received those long surveys that are full of questions with little tick boxes next to them? They ask you things like:

- What make of car do you drive?
- What newspaper do you read?
- Which of the following magazines do you read? (Choose from a list)

- Do you have house contents insurance?
- Where do you usually shop?
  (They give you a list to choose from)
- Which of these brands of cigarettes do you smoke? (Another list)
- Do you belong to a fitness club?
- Are you a tenant or do you own your house?
- Which of the following describes your income bracket? (Another list)
- What is your age group? (Another list)

If you have seen these surveys then you will know what I'm talking about. Once again you may get told that by filling in the survey and posting it off you will be entered into a free prize draw for a holiday in the sun. Testicles!

If you fill in and send off these surveys then you could be signing yourself up to be profiled. If they receive a number of forms from the same post code area they are able to build up a profile of that area that can have an adverse effect on people's credit rating and property value in that area.

Don't be taken in by these things. You maybe sent one of these forms from a company that you have dealings with and they might inform you that the reason for the survey is to supply a better service to you as one of their highly valued customers. This is testicles. You will find out how highly valued you are when you phone them up and get told that if you would like to speak to an advisor you are eighth in the queue.

From these surveys they can work out the average age group and income bracket of your area. They will be able to tell the average age of cars in your area. They will know what newspapers are read by the people in your area, tabloids or broadsheets. They will know how many people are likely to have or not have house contents insurance. Do you see the bigger picture? Throw all surveys and questionnaires into the dustbin. Don't give out information that can be used against you.

Many of the big stores and supermarkets now have Loyalty Reward Cards. Why do you suppose that is? Could it be because most of them now supply loans, credit cards, store cards and insurance? By giving you about 1p in every pound you spend the store knows what products you use, clothes you and members of your family wear, whether or not you or someone in your family smokes. If you buy newspapers or magazines at the same store they will know about them too. The sizes of clothes and shoes you buy will give them an idea as to how many adults and children are likely to be in your household. If you pay for your shopping with a debit or credit card it will tell them who you bank with or who your credit card is supplied by. Seeing they have your details, that you very kindly supplied to them when applying for your reward card, you and the area you live in are likely to be profiled.

Can you see why I said (Chapter 3) that the government could be moving towards getting rid of cash? It would give them control over everyone.

If you don't want to be profiled then don't fill in surveys and questionnaires. Perform plastic surgery on your loyalty reward cards with a pair of scissors and draw money out of "the hole in the wall" and pay for your shopping with cash.

If you can, try and cut up those credit cards and store cards as well. They have become the bane of people's lives and can be a very expensive way of getting yourself profiled and your movements monitored.

Did you know that if you have a credit card with a £2000 credit limit on it and you take the card to the limit and make only the minimum monthly payment on the outstanding amount it will take you over thirty years to pay it off and you will pay back over £8000? What was it that you needed so desperately at the time that you were prepared to pay so much money for? Where will that thing be when you make your final payment? It's much the same as buying that new car and paying all that interest on it.

People visit a car show room and often leave with a £14,000 or more debt. They buy a car for about £9,000 and about another £5,000 in interest gets added onto it. The moment the car is driven out of the show room it drops in value. Do you see why people are retiring broke and often broken? It's not just because of all the tax that the government take from them; it's also because they have spent their lives making others wealthy.

Recently a friend of mine was out shopping and he was using one of those credit cards to make some purchases. The third time he used the card his mobile phone rang in the store, he answered it but no one spoke, he checked the menu for a number but it had been with-held. He was being watched on CCTV and contacted to see if he was the person who should have the card. He had supplied his mobile number when he made the application for the credit card.

There is another kind of questionnaire and survey that local service providers may send to people. These are ones that they use to congratulate themselves with because the results will show that they are performing well, reaching targets and that 98% of people who used their services were happy with the service they received. They use very selective questions for these surveys. Why do they need to do these things anyway? Is it to justify their existence?

DON'T SWALLOW THE TESTICLES

Keep ownership of your mind. Stop being so helpful and make ALL Surveys, Questionnaires and Loyalty Reward Cards REDUNDANT.

10
So You're In Love, Are You?

Let's start by asking ourselves, what is a relationship? We all have relationships with other people whether it be within the family, the work place, our social activities, our neighbours, our friends at school or college and of course with our partners. I want to focus on the relationship between partners, that modern term that seems to have replaced wife, husband and fiancé.

Let's return to that Garden of Eden once again. If this Adam and Eve were the first two people then it looks as if man and woman's behaviour hasn't changed very much. We are told in the story (mature view) that God caught Adam scrumping apples and when challenged Adam said, "It wasn't my fault, that woman made me do it". God then went to Eve and her story was that "It was the snakes fault". The poor snake, of course, didn't have a leg to stand on. Down the years man has blamed woman for his own unhappy state and woman has blamed man (the snake/penis) for her own unhappiness.

It seems almost the norm today to be engaged more times than some telephones and married at least three times by the time you're forty. I believe one reason for this is that men and women are getting married too young. I believe that a woman should be between 25 – 30 before she gets married and a man should be in his seventies. I believe that a man will be more settled within himself at this age.

DON'T SWALLOW THE TESTICLES

What is this thing called love that has driven people to do desperate acts? Does anyone know what love is? I've heard some weird and sick interpretations and definitions of it. I've seen people expressing their love for each other by having rows and fights. People have killed in its name. Most people have sex in the name of love. Thousands of songs and books have been written about love and hundreds of films made, but what is this thing called love?

I believe that I love my daughter Kate. I have thoughts and feelings for her that I have never had for another human being. I believe that I would kill and die for her. Perhaps my present feelings for her are because she is so young and vulnerable and in need of protection. At this time she is learning to walk and talk but each time I look at her I get a most wonderful feeling wash over me.

There have been a number of times in my life when I thought that I was in love but I have to say that never once did I experience the joy I feel when I see my daughter.

I believe that many relationships start with a period of intense sex followed by a cooling off period followed by a pissed off period. The sex might be the kind that involves the man telling the woman to say "fuck me" and all kinds of other verbal obscenities. Many women probably don't need cueing as they may already be familiar with the pornographic minds of most men. I've always thought that there is something concrete about the words "fuck me". When the sex act is finished it is time to reach for the tissues to wipe the bits and pieces with and then drop the wet tissues down the side of the bed onto the floor. Some couples like a fag and to talk a load of testicles at this time; others, or perhaps the man, might just want to go to sleep. Have you noticed how hard those tissues are when they dry? You could make models with them when they are still wet and then paint them when they are dry. I'm just passing on this little creative idea in case you are looking to take up a new hobby.

Have you ever been in bed with a woman who asks you to hold her while she has a DIY orgasm? This can be very wearisome especially if you have had your orgasm and just want to go to sleep. Are there any women in the world who are like men and can have their orgasm during sexual intercourse? It can be very inconvenient when they want to catch up afterwards.

For years the sex act has been referred to as "making love". This is a polite term for blow jobs, tongue baths, doggies, 69s and the verbal that can go on during the act. The term was probably thought up by the aristocracy because it sounds so much nicer if one is discussing sex in ones own circles.

I don't believe that love and sex are one and the same thing. I believe that they need to be separated out. Many couples would like to believe that their children were conceived from acts of love. They may have been, but they may also have been conceived from drunken bouts of sex, one night stands or an attempt to save a failing relationship.

If a couple met and spent a year or so really getting to know each other, without having sex, they may find that after that period of time they might not want to have sex because it could ruin what they have. After that length of time without sex they would both probably have white sticks. Sex moves the emotional goal posts and jealousy and possessiveness are born. When this happens many couples become like the characters seen in those TV soaps. What they have produced is not a recipe for happiness but rather a recipe for misery.

DON'T SWALLOW THE TESTICLES

I've tried to explain in simple terms what I believe love isn't. Let's now move on and try and establish what it is.

If we earnestly desire a true lifelong relationship with another human being then we first must face one of the greatest challenges ever known. We need to first seek a divorce, from ourselves. Until this mountain is climbed there is little hope of complete fulfilment from a close and loving relationship.

Of course, if we wait until this feat is accomplished before going into a relationship we will be very old and probably won't even have taken the first step towards it. I think that this mountain can be conquered by two people climbing together. The two are probably quite different, they maybe from different backgrounds, have different views on life, different ways of doing things, different values and different ideas about what a relationship should be like. I am not talking here about becoming self-sacrificing; I am talking about overcoming self-centredness. It is self-centredness that causes us to control and manipulate others in order that we can have things the way that we want them.

This self-centredness is a serious matter. We all have it or it has us. Wouldn't everything be just wonderful if everyone did exactly as we wanted them to? But they don't, do they? They go and do things their way without even consulting us. Now that really is self-centred behaviour on their part. How on earth can you help people when they behave like that?

Love is not doing things for others. Doing things for others might just be another attempt to control them. I might buy presents and do great deeds so that they will think of me as being kind and considerate and a good chap, but why would I need them to think of me in this way?

I've met many people who have changed themselves in the

hope of being accepted by their so-called friends. One particular lady told me that her friends would say to each other, behind her back, "She would be so much better if only she would change her style of clothes". She eventually realised that these people were not real friends and that she didn't need them in her life. What a huge growth step that was for her. Did these friends love her, of course they didn't.

Real friends accept you exactly as you are, they would never do anything to try to change you. A real friend though would stand in your way if they believed that you were on a self-destruct course. If you find two such friends in your lifetime then you will have done very well indeed. The trick in life is not to make a friend but to be a friend. It is about unclenching the fist and holding out the hand. If two people are pulling at each end of a piece of string the string will soon break, if one person lets go of the string it won't.

So, have we discovered yet what this thing called love is? I don't believe that we have. I'm not convinced that we know what real love is. I once heard it described as the unselfish concern for another human being, I'm not convinced if that is totally achievable.

Much of this stuff that gets called love is testicles. Is it romance? No, romance is not love. Is it a love affair? No, it's not that either. There has always been this tendency to link love with sex and I don't believe that it has anything to do with sex. Sex is linked to lust not to love. I believe that many relationships end when the couple fall out of lust. That well known statement, "You don't love me anymore" could be read as you don't lust after me anymore. Sex is a very powerful force and it can be used to control and manipulate. Careers have been ruined and lives ended because of sex.

DON'T SWALLOW THE TESTICLES

There are women who have discovered that the only way they can get their partner to buy a new washing machine or anything else for the home is by depriving him of sex. When the new washing machine or whatever appears it's like saying "abracadabra" and her legs move back to twenty past eight again. There are couples that go on like this for years. The bloke would be better of having a polish and buying her a rubber husband; it would be a lot less expensive.

Love probably can't be defined. If someone tells you that they love you there is no way that you can disprove that person's claim. You could say, "Prove it, jump through hoops of fire for me" but this would not prove that persons love for you. Why would you need proof anyway?

We need to get rid of all the testicles that surround emotionally charged relationships. Firstly, you must realise that you will be attracted to a particular type of person for whatever reason. Why do some women go for drunks? Why do some go for criminals? Why do some go for abusers? Why do some go for older men? Why do some go for publicity junkies? The truth is no one knows, so forget all the theories. I only know what chocolate cake tastes like for me; I have no idea what it tastes like for you.

When you are first attracted to someone you are really attracted to the image of that person and not to the actual person themselves. If a relationship develops between you both then you may reveal yourselves to each other, but in most cases these revelations will only be at surface level. This means that they will be revealed as habits, likes and dislikes. You may reveal what's in your minds but not what's in your hearts. Failing to reveal what's in your hearts will ensure that you remain intimate strangers.

DON'T SWALLOW THE TESTICLES

The longest journey a human being will make is only about sixteen or so inches long. It is the journey from ones head to ones heart. The heart of another human being can be like the sun, impossible to reach and you will get burnt if you try to.

Being attracted to an image of someone is probably best demonstrated by what many people do with these so-called celebrities. They see them on TV, in newspapers and magazines and they may have pictures and calendars of them on the walls in their homes but they don't know them and may have never met them, yet for some strange reason they adore them. It is quite possible that if they did get to know them they might quickly find themselves going off them.

There are so many sayings about love. "Falling in Love", "You always hurt the one you Love", "True love never dies", "True love never runs smooth".

I believe these sayings have nothing to do with love. In the card shops recently were all the Valentine Cards. The words in these cards are gush and also have nothing to do with love. Many of these cards get sent to people anonymously, sent to people who are fancied by someone, that's not love. I've sent these cards myself to women I fancied shagging not loving.

There is another old saying about losing your head over someone. Don't lose your head over anyone. Don't give someone else ownership of your mind, it is very irresponsible.

11
If You Keep Doing What You're Doing You'll Keep Getting What You're Getting

One morning an elderly couple who had been together for over fifty years got up out of bed and the man said to the woman, "Lets do something really exciting and different tonight" and having said that he went downstairs. The woman stayed in the bedroom and began to think about what the man had said. She thought, "I wonder what he's got planned". "Perhaps he's going to take me out for a meal or maybe to the theatre"; "I'll pop into town and get my hair done just in case and while I'm there I might buy a new dress". She eventually went downstairs and the man was sat at the breakfast table having a cup of tea. She said, "Well, what is it that you have in mind to do tonight that will be really exciting and different"? The man replied, "I thought we might swap armchairs". (Author Unknown)

For many people that is how it is, the same old routine. Do you change chairs in your house or do you have your chair that the rest of the family dare not sit in. When I was a kid my mother was always telling us, "Don't sit there, that's your fathers chair". What a load of testicles, though at the time it was a wise thing not to sit in his chair.

DON'T SWALLOW THE TESTICLES

Are you a tree rooted to the ground? Is there barbed wire and guard dogs preventing you from leaving your home or your job or your area? Are you in an unhappy relationship and allowing fear and guilt to prevent you from getting out of it? What's the difference between someone spending their life in prison and someone spending their life on the outside? For many people the answer is, there is very little difference. Prison can be a state of mind and that is why it is so important to have ownership of yours. There are people locked up who are free and there are people who are free who are locked up.

Are you happy? If I asked you to tell me the happiest person that you know, who would it be? Would you name yourself as that person? If not, why not? Is there any area of your life that you are not satisfied with? If there is, what have you done to change it? Where do you see yourself five years from now? Do you think that your future is something that you should be addressing today? What do you think would have happened if Noah had decided to wait for the rain before he built the Ark? If things don't change they will stay as they are. The biggest room in the world is the room for improvement.

In the introduction to this book I said that the message that I have is that "Misery is Optional" and I really believe that to be so. We manufacture our own misery because misery is a state of mind. We love to blame others for all the shit that happens in our lives but we must take responsibility for what we think and feel. Yes, someone may do something that offends us and we may well experience feelings of resentment towards that person, we may even want to shake hands with their windpipe, but if we are still feeling like that after a couple of weeks then that is our problem not theirs. I'm talking here about the day to day trifle things like someone gossiping about us or the job or the boss is getting to us or someone cuts us up on the road; life's little mole hills that can get turned into mountains.

Some people waste years of their life hating someone else. Sadly, hate will ultimately destroy the hater. I knew someone who often tried to tell me that she will never forgive a certain person for what they did to her. Every opportunity she gets to fan the flames of her resentment and drip her poison about this person she takes up with gusto. It has been going on for over twenty years and she cannot see that the one she has poisoned is herself. For all those years she has had constant bad health and rather than see the connection between that and her resentment over this person she blames that person for her health problems as well. I somehow feel that the other person is probably unaware of all this and sleeping soundly every night.

I've made a number of references in this book to CHANGE. Why do you suppose that is? Unless we open our eyes and look to see where we are and where we really would like to be then we will continue to keep doing what we're doing. I do not believe that we are in this world to suffer and to crawl through life and end up with nothing. ***The tramp sat on the park bench and watched the wealthy man drive past in a Rolls Royce and the tramp said to himself, "There but for me go I".*** (Author Unknown).

One of the many things I have learnt is that it isn't change that is painful; it's resistance to change that's painful. Like many others I had to be brought to a point in life where it was a choice of change or face the consequences. I was offered a way out of a life that I had come to accept as normal. Today I know that way of life was abnormal. It always seemed right to do the wrong thing. My vision of life was blurred. I always thought that I was having a great time but really it was all testicles. I always had like minded people around me and I thought that they were great guys. It is many years since I have seen or spoken to any of them. It was best that we parted company. If you escape from the lions den you don't go back for your hat. I came to believe that it is no use being on a new path with old ideas.

Whenever I have spoken to a gathering of people I have always asked each one of them the question: "Who are you? Not what are you"? Go and look in your mirror and look yourself in the eyes and ask yourself that question. Ask yourself what you are doing here and what are you doing with your life.

The marketing gurus have created a yearly commercial plan of testicles for us to follow. It is a spend, spend, spend plan. For most people it has turned into a debt, debt, debt plan.

The plan consist of Valentines Day, Mother's Day, Easter, Father's Day, The Boss's Day, The Secretary's Day, Grand Mother's Day, Grand Father's Day, Birthdays, Fireworks Night, Christmas, After Christmas Sales, New Years Celebrations, Spring Sales, Summer Sales, Autumn Sales, Winter Sales, Blue Cross Day, Special Offers Day, Do you get the picture?

Many people have allowed themselves to buy into all this load of testicles. Just before last Christmas I walked through my home City Centre and I couldn't see one thing in the shops that was absolutely necessary. Now, before you call me "Scrooge" I want you to know that I did buy some presents. Personally, I couldn't give a fuck whether High Street spending is up or down. When they announce on TV that it is down I don't feel that I have to rush out and help to push it up.

It never ceases to amaze me that so many people rush out to these sales and buy things they don't really need in order to save money. They then pay for these things with credit cards and store cards that they are probably going to pay interest on. I know a couple who spent a whole day at the sales. They had a taxi take them to the shops, they had lunch whilst they were there and they had a taxi back home. Everything they bought was paid for with a credit card. How much do you think they saved that day?

Some months ago I read of a man who had committed suicide because of all the debt that he had incurred. Following his death his widow found a large number of credit cards hidden away on top of a wardrobe. Suicide is a permanent solution to a temporary problem. If you are in debt don't take that course of action. When you are in a hole the number one rule is to immediately stop digging. That means cut up all the credit and store cards and cancel the direct debits and standing orders. The name of the game now is survival.

Firstly, you must ensure that you pay your rent or mortgage because you need a roof over your head. Secondly, write to your creditors and ask them to freeze the interest on your account and agree a pay back plan with them. Don't borrow more money to try to pay off your debts; you will never break free from debt if you do.

Debt has become another industry and there are people out there who will be only too happy to help you, for a price. Keep away from these people. Don't be frightened by threats of legal action and of people being sent to your home. It is not a crime to owe money. It is a crime to dishonestly obtain money. Make sure that you pay those bills that they can send bailiffs to your home for the non payment of. Council Tax and Parking Fines are two of them. A file will be opened on you at Credit Reference Agencies and you will not be able to get any more credit. If you see those adverts for loans that say "Bad Debt, CCJ's, Defaults, No Problem" ignore them, they will want you to send them a so-called fee and then they will refer you to lenders who will run a check on you with the Credit Reference Agencies and you will be right back to where you started.

Today many people have things in their homes that were once considered luxuries of the rich. Recently I listened to a known about hair stylist who said that quite often ordinary people came to their salon and paid £500 to get their hair done just for the experience. It probably makes them feel like a millionaire for an hour. It's not something that I would do myself. I can get forty five haircuts for that money at my hairdressers.

Do you fancy a walk? Take a jaunt around your local cemetery. Yes I know that it's not exactly an enjoyable event but this is just a fact finding tour. Look at some of the gravestones and see what they say on them. Does it say what the guy had done for a living? Does it say what football team he had supported? Does it say what political party he had voted for? Does it say what kind of car he had driven? Does it say if he had been a millionaire? Does it say what sort of house he had lived in? Does it say where he had spent his holidays? Does it say what hairdresser he had used? Does it say what schools he had attended? Does it say that he had come from a dysfunctional family? Does it say what his religion had been? Does it say what colour he had been? Do you see what it is that I am trying to convey to you?

Why is so much emphasis placed on these things whilst we are here walking around on top of the ground?

During one period of my life I was asked to inter someone's ashes and I remember holding the urn and thinking, "Gosh this only weighs about the same as a bag of sugar". That experience served to put many things into perspective for me and suddenly some of the things that had seemed important became unimportant.

The marketing gurus have tried to design our lives for us but we need to design our own lives. Don't try to live a wealthy life style if you are not wealthy. The weight of debt will have a miserable effect on you. Make sure that everything is okay on the inside your house otherwise the lovely garden on the outside will only be a mask.

Now, unfortunately we do live in a "rat race" today and society is divided into two categories. There are predators and prey. Which one are you?

I believe that we are probably all predators but we very often allow ourselves to become prey. Those people who allow themselves to be controlled are really the ones doing the controlling. Those who allow themselves to be dominated are doing the dominating. If you want to escape the "rat race" then stop being a rat, it's that simple.

We are living in an age where we have so many time saving gadgets and yet so little time. Everyone seems to be busy, busy, busy. It's now 24/7. Open all hours. More houses are now built in Closes and Cul-de-Sacs and people can now walk through their home into their garage and get into their car and drive out to a Supermarket on the outskirts of their town and buy everything they need and drive back home again. They don't need to talk to anyone, not even their neighbours. I believe that people are becoming more and more isolated from each other and that all this buying that they do is an attempt to fix a sense of inner loneliness. I also believe that because there is a breakdown in social communication it has made many people hostile towards others.

Text messaging and emailing have replaced real communication. I believe one of the most common used words today is the word Hi. Every time I get an email or a text it starts with Hi Kevin. Whatever happened to the word Dear? Text and emails are okay I suppose but they can't give someone a hug, they don't put an arm around someone and say everything's going to be alright. I've seen youngsters in the streets with mobiles stuck to their ears! One lady told me that she had to take the mobile away from her daughter because one month's bill for it was over £80. Her daughter would even text all her friends when a certain song came on the radio that she wanted them to hear.

When I set out on my journey of recovery and discovery almost twenty four years ago one of my friends said to me, "Life is a simple thing for complicated people". Today I know what those words mean. I totally believe that life is to be enjoyed and not endured. Enjoyment of life should be the biggest addiction of our times. Did you know that fewer facial muscles are used by laughing than are used by scowling? So keep laughing and you won't need any of that face cream to cover up frown lines.

I've so enjoyed sharing my beliefs with you and I hope that they are of some help in your own journey through this thing called life. Just tell yourself when you get up each morning that something great is going to happen to you today. Be nice to everyone you meet (even politicians and publicity junkies) and if you are not enjoying your life then go to the mirror and say to yourself,

You Are Now Looking At The Problem.

Notes

Notes

Notes

Notes

ISBN 1-41204554-1